THE SHAPING OF THE COUNTRYSIDE

THE SHAPING OF THE COUNTRYSIDE

by

Ralph Whitlock

ROBERT HALE · LONDON

ISBN 0 7091 7371 7

Robert Hale Limited
Clerkenwell House
Clerkenwell Green
London, EC1

Photoset by
Specialised Offset Services, Liverpool
Printed in Great Britain by
Lowe & Brydone, Thetford

Contents

Illustrations

PICTURE CREDITS
Ben Darby: no 1, 2, 3, 5, 6, 8, 10, 12, 20, 25, 28, 30, 33, 34, 36, 39, 40; Geoffrey N. Wright: no 4, 7, 9, 11, 13, 14, 15, 16, 17, 18, 19, 21, 22, 23, 24, 26, 27, 29, 32, 35, 37, 38; Richard Jemmett: no 31

1

At The Beginning

A neighbour in the Wiltshire village where I was born remarked to me in about the year 1955, when the influx of newcomers was beginning to assume formidable proportions,

"What a pity we can't keep the place just as it used to be!"

I instinctively agreed with him, but a regard for accuracy made me temper my reply, with a smile to soothe the sting, with

"If we could, you wouldn't be here!"

For he was one of the first batch of newcomers, who had moved in just before the Second World War.

Since then I have more than once heard the same complaint from subsequent immigrants. Each one, having chosen the charming village for residence (in many instances, for retirement) because of its obvious attractions, has naturally wanted to preserve those attractions. Having occupied new villas on the sites of demolished cottages or having altered a surviving cottage almost beyond recognition, they have engaged in local politics with the aim of preventing any further building development. They illustrate the very human desire to stop the clock at a convenient moment. When a glorious sunset is the climax of a perfect summer day, we wish that time would stand still. We would like the honeymoon to be prolonged indefinitely. In our sixties we look forward to qualifying for our retirement pension, but when that date arrives, finding us still healthy and active, we long for the power to stop there and not drift downhill into the seventies and eighties. That we can achieve a state of perfect rest and escape the course of change is an illusion.

Before the present century, the pace of change in the countryside was slower. The village referred to above was said to be the stronghold of three families, the Whites, Whitlocks and Collinses. There they are, occupying most of the pages of the parish registers back to the 1650s, when the earliest begins. They must have comprised at least half the village population for several centuries. But lawsuits and other documents relating to the place in the Middle Ages mention none of those names. There was a time, evidently, when none of the three families lived there. All were newcomers, equally with those who arrived in the 1950s, 1960s and 1970s.

For more than forty years, when the leaves fell and the crops were harvested, I turned with my spade the soil of my garden. As far as can be ascertained, the house in which I was born was built in that garden by my great-grandfather, or perhaps my great-grandfather's father. So at least four generations of my family must have spent the October days thrusting the spade into that same familiar plot. Now the task falls to other hands. Before the time of the Whitlocks the garden existed and was cultivated by gardeners now forgotten as completely as the worms which I disturbed by my annual activities, and as I shall be when a sufficient cycle of years has passed.

The garden and the house were constructed on what was evidently an ancient green track, linking who knows what termini. In the 1950s someone digging a cess-pit just along the road discovered a burial. The skeleton, pronounced the archaeologists who examined it, was of a man who had passed that way when Stonehenge was new. His foot had trod the turf that covered the spot where my garden was to be 3,500 years later. Probably he would have gazed at Stonehenge, which is less than ten miles away. Did he shake his head in disapproval, deploring the changes typified by the erection of such a monstrous structure?

Where, then, does one begin when approaching the theme of 'the Shaping of the Countryside'? To find a fixed point, about which one can say, "Here Change began," is an impossibility. Logically, we could probe back into geological time. We could start in the Eocene era, when the clays and heaths of the London Basin were laid down by mighty, silt-laden rivers pouring into a sea that extended to the east of what is now Britain. Or we could venture back further, into the Cretaceous period, when the chalk downs which form immense, petrified waves rolling in parallels diagonally across England, were the flat bed of a shallow sea bordered by a desert continent. We might even explore in the earliest ages, when the crust of the infant earth was slowly solidifying over a molten sea of magma and when spouting volcanoes dominated a landscape not yet clothed in green.

Our canvas must be more restricted. We cannot do justice to the 4,700 million years that have elapsed since the earth was first launched as a fiery ball into space. Nor can we take stock of the 3,000 million years that have passed since the first primitive forms of life appeared on our planet. Even the occurrence of the first traces of man is too far remote, in both time and space, for they have been found in Africa and date from five million years ago. Britain then had in its still distant future to endure at least three long Ice Ages before it could become a congenial habitat for men.

The latest theories allow the Ice Ages a period of from around 590,000 BC to 12,000 BC, each of the three major glaciations being followed by a long warm intermission (of from 60,000 to 190,000 years). The first men of whom any trace has been found were in Britain (in Kent) about 250,000 years ago. As the Ice Ages advanced and retreated, so men advanced or retired with the frontiers of the ice. Thus, although the advent of man in Britain can be put back to a quarter of a million years ago, there must have been long subsequent periods when, for reasons of climate, the country was uninhabited and unhabitable.

The last ice cap, similar to those now blanketing Greenland and Antarctica, extended southwards over the greater part of Britain to the edge of the Thames valley. For a long way south of the limits of the ice the land must have been highly inhospitable tundra, much like the wastes of northern Canada. Then, unpredictably, the ice began to recede. As the centuries passed, the tundra gradually gave way to conifer forests, then to deciduous woodland and pastures. To imagine vast herds of elk, aurochs, mammoth and other herbivorous mammals grazing on the tundra and later on the meadows and parkland is legitimate. Probably a great northward migration occurred each spring, with a corresponding southward ebb in autumn. Most likely they were harassed by, among other parasitic predators, our early ancestors.

Our islands were, of course, not islands in those days. The advance of the waters to cover the plains of the North Sea and the English Channel occurred only after the glaciers had melted and caused a huge rise in sea level. Tools and other evidences of prehistoric men have been dredged up from the Dogger Bank, in the central area of the North Sea. The severance of the last land bridge with the continent of Europe, as the sea poured through the Straits of Dover to complete our 'moat defensive', found men already well established on the hither side.

Here, then, is where we will start. The numbers of humans resident in Britain in the interglacial periods and even as late as the formation of the Straits must have been very small, perhaps only a few hundred individuals. They could have had only an infinitesimal impact on their environment. It is only with the beginning of farming in Neolithic times, somewhere between 3,000 and 2,000 BC that man began to effect noticeable changes in the landscape.

Once again, as we begin to look more closely at the countryside which these tiny groups of humans were in due course to transform into the habitat we know, we find ourselves in an age of transition. Indeed, some authorities maintain that changes were occurring quite rapidly, due largely to an amelioration of the climate caused by the transformation of Britain into an island. The breaching of the Straits of Dover, according to this school of thought, allowed the warm currents of the Atlantic ready access to the cold North Sea. Certainly about the year 3,500 BC Britain entered into a warm, damp Atlantic period.

We cannot then assume that the appearance of the countryside was much the same as it would be today if no men had ever come to our shores. Since those balmy days of warm summers and Atlantic breezes, Britain has experienced several periods of deterioration of climate, notably in the first millennium BC. Much of the area now covered with deep layers of peat was forest or open grassland when our Neolithic ancestors first investigated it.

However, then as now Britain could be broadly divided into two main regions, a Highland and a Lowland zone. A diagonal line from the coast of county Durham to the mouth of the Exe is the approximate boundary between the two, though with the gap of the Cheshire and Lancashire Plain separating the Pennines from the mountains of Wales and allowing the lowlands of Midland England access to the Irish Sea. Highland Britain thus comprises all of Scotland, the mountains and hills of Cumbria and the Pennines, all of Wales and the south-western peninsula. The distinction between the two zones is accentuated by the fact that the Highland is composed largely of the older, harder rocks, while the newer and softer measures are in the Lowlands.

Yet in those far-off halcyon days there was less difference between Highland and Lowland than there is at present. Now we are down to the nude. Over most of the country the landscape has been stripped of its natural covering and stands bare and exposed for all to see its structure. Then it was densely clad in an overcoat of forests wherever trees could take root.

Those great forests endured into historical times. We are familiar with the early mediaeval claim that a squirrel could travel from the Severn estuary to The Wash without ever once leaving the tree-tops. There are intriguing references in early documents to the great Caledonian Forest and the fearsome animals, such as wild bulls, wolves, elk and bears, that lurked in its depths. The Wealden Forest in Kent and Sussex was so dense and difficult that men made little impact on it until Tudor times.

Neolithic men, with only stone tools, tended to avoid the forest. They settled on the uplands, above the tree line, and on coastal glades and pastures and on soils too thin to support trees. As it happened, they were apparently dauntless seafarers. Evidence seems to point to at least one wave of migrants arriving in Britain across the seas to the south-west. The Orkneys, the Hebrides and the west coasts of Scotland seem to have been as thickly populated in Neolithic times as the south-eastern shores of England.

There was one region, however, which lent itself ideally to human movement and settlement, and that was the broad belt of chalk and limestone measures which stretches diagonally across England from East Yorkshire to Dorset. From Midland England this zone bulges eastwards to include much of East Anglia; from its southern node in Wiltshire and Hampshire, it thrusts out long arms eastwards, on either side of The Weald, to reach the sea at points conveniently situated opposite the nearest shores of continental Europe. The North Downs, the

South Downs and the Dorset Downs therefore became natural highways for generations of traders and settlers from the Continent. As a bonus, the chalk downs were also the source of the most highly-prized raw material of the Neolithic era, flint.

In our imagination we can walk with a group of those first Neolithic explorers of this new and attractive land. We are travelling on the hill crests, where soft, springy turf makes walking easy. The children can race and gambol and fall without hurting themselves. A mild yet bracing breeze from the south-west chases a procession of cottony white clouds across a pale blue sky. Lapwings and stone-curlew, disturbed by the unfamiliar intruders, rise with loud protests; wheatears flirt their white tail-patches and perch on old ant nests to survey the newcomers; overhead, larks unwind their continuous chain of song. Down in the valleys unbroken forests extend as far as the eye can see. In places the trees, like a mighty green tide, come lapping at the edges of the downland prairie. Here the children with delight find sulphur-coloured primroses to pick. Inside the woods they can see tempting displays of bluebells and wood anemones, but their parents summon back any venturesome enough to enter. For the woods are filled with mysterious dangers. The wild cattle which they could see far off earlier in the day and when fled at their approach have taken refuge among the trees, and a fierce and formidable bull may be lurking in any thicket. Wolves, bears and lynxes are to be expected anywhere past the forest fringe. There may be some of those small, dark, hairy men whom some wayfarers profess to have seen. And, of course, the forest is thickly peopled with sprites and spirits, as their wise men have asserted for many generations. The secret, twilight world beneath the trees is a place to be avoided. Better to stay in the open, where a man's eyes can give warning of danger.

Yet this is a lovely land. The summers are warm, the winters mild. Game is abundant, and the thin upland soils are easily cultivated. What more can a tribe, seeking a place to settle, ask for? This is a good place to call home.

2

The Prehistoric Contribution

We may be excused for regarding prehistoric men as energetic moles. They were great at moving quantities of earth. Silbury Hill, for instance, which is said to be the largest artificial mound of earth in Europe, was made by them. It is 125–30 feet high, approximately 550 feet in diameter at the base, and covers about 5½ acres. The chalk downs in the vicinity are spangled with barrows, or tumuli, many of which resemble Silbury in miniature.

The men of prehistory also constructed imposing earthworks on the crests of hills. The earlier and simpler ramparts may have been planned as mere cattle corrals; the later and more elaborate ones were undoubtedly military fortifications. Many of these hill-top fortresses enclose areas of from ten to forty acres. Maiden Castle, in Dorset, one of the largest and latest of them, was a fully-fledged town and still has ramparts eighty feet high. These must have been crowned, when the place was inhabited, by massive timber fortifications.

Prehistoric men handled stone with equal confidence. The generally accepted theory of how the 'blue stones' of Stonehenge were brought from the Prescelly Mountains of Pembrokeshire is now quite well known. It asserts that the stones were ferried across the Bristol Channel on rafts, which were then towed up the Bristol Avon, pushed on wooden rollers over the portage to the headwaters of the River Wylye, down which they were floated on another raft to the confluence of that river with the Salisbury Avon, and finally northwards up the Avon to the nearest point to the site, two miles away over the downs. Though the task was formidable, the 'blue stones' are among the lesser ones which comprise

Stonehenge. They weigh about five tons each, whereas the sarsen stones of the original edifice are of about twenty-five tons, and the huge uprights that support the lintels of the trilithons weigh up to forty-five tons. They had not so far to travel, probably from the Marlborough Downs, twenty miles away, but inching them down on rollers must have been a colossal undertaking. That the feat is possible has been demonstrated in recent times by groups of students who moved similar stones by similar methods. However, it is intriguing to note that the mediaeval writer (romancer, as some would call him) Geoffrey of Monmouth, attributes the moving of the stones to the magician Merlin, who, he said, "burst out laughing" when he saw an army of men using "hawsers, ropes and scaling ladders" without success. When it was his turn to try, "he put together his own engines, laid the stones down so lightly as none would believe, and bade them carry them to the ships". I find it interesting that the story speaks of mechanical means rather than magic spells. Geoffrey of Monmouth was a notorious mixer of fact with fancy, but there are indications that he did have access to some sources of information that have since been lost. Incidentally, he makes the stones come from Ireland, not Pembrokeshire.

Circles and other edifices of standing stones are to be found in many parts of Britain. Avebury, some twenty miles north of Stonehenge, is one of the largest and is linked by a sinuous avenue, marked by standing stones, to a mysterious circle, known as The Sanctuary, on a hill a mile-and-a-half away. Stanton Drew, on the hills above Bath, consists of three circles of stones six feet high, the largest circle having a diameter of 368 feet, and again there is an avenue leading from it. Stone circles of impressive size occur as far north as the Outer Hebrides, where the Isle of Lewis has the great circle and avenue of Callernish, and Stenness in Orkney.

The erection of stone monuments of such stature implies the existence of a considerable population, and one, moreover, sufficiently well organized to allow for leisure-time to be used in such work. Some authorities would credit the builders with even more startling achievements. Professor Gerald S. Hawkins, of the Smithsonian Astrophysical Observatory at Cambridge, Massachusetts, startled the world in 1966 with his book *Stonehenge Decoded*, in which, with the aid of a computer, he pointed out that the stones and post-holes of Stonehenge could be used as a primitive computer, to predict eclipses and other astronomical phenomena. If he is correct, and many think he is, the men who constructed it must have had an advanced knowledge of astronomy and mathematics.

It is at this point that we should remind ourselves of the chronology of the period with which we are dealing. Prehistory is generally agreed to be the period of time before the compilation of written records, which, for Britain, began with the arrival of the Romans in the first century BC and the first century AD. As our story begins, by definition in Chapter 1, at around 3,500 BC, we are dealing with an expanse of about 3,500 years, about the same length of time as divides us from the builders of Stonehenge. While there were perhaps not as many cataclysmic changes in the period 3,500 BC to 1 BC as there have been between Stonehenge and the twentieth century AD, it is reasonable to suppose that many changes did occur. The same peoples were not responsible for every prehistoric feature which adorns our landscape.

After the first Neolithic farming folk settled in Britain, new groups frequently arrived from overseas to stake out a place in the richly-endowed island. At first their coming was peaceful, for there was plenty of room for all. Later, as the country became more crowded, the newcomers appeared as warlike invaders. They often had the advantage of advanced techniques and weapons, derived from emerging civilizations in the Mediterranean region and the East, which enabled them to chase away the resident tribes into the forests or mountains or to enslave them. Thus people with bronze weapons and tools superseded those with a purely Stone Age culture. In their turn, the warriors who relied on bronze swords and daggers were defeated by newcomers who had learned the secret of working iron.

Bronze was introduced to Britain about 1800 BC by invaders known to archaeologists as 'the Beaker Folk', after their characteristic pottery. They arrived in several waves, over two or three centuries, and created what seems to have been a brilliant aristocracy in southern England. It was they who refashioned Stonehenge, already existing in rudimentary form, and left their trademark on one of the stones in the form of carvings of a bronze dagger and bronze axe-heads. There is evidence that they traded with Greece, Egypt and other countries of the Mediterranean world.

Archaeologists date the Bronze Age in Britain from about 1800 BC to about 550 BC. Throughout that long period trade and prosperity seem gradually to have increased, and in the final centuries more and more settlers arrived from the Continent, bringing with them new ideas and techniques. Among other innovations was a new type of plough, drawn by oxen, which replaced primitive digging-sticks, as well as new types of pottery and metalware.

550 BC is the approximate date for the introduction of iron and the beginning of the Iron Age. At first the iron-users were small groups of settlers from north-eastern France, but later invasions were in greater strength, and the invaders came as conquerors. This is the age of the Celts, that abundant people who once occupied the greater part of Europe north of the Alps and who were strong enough to capture and sack Rome in 390 BC. By 55 BC, when Caesar's reconnaissance opened a window on British affairs to the Roman world, Celts were well established in a group of independent kingdoms from Dorset to Yorkshire, with tribes of earlier arrivals in the territories to the west. There were exceptions to this general pattern, as, for instance, in the south-western peninsula, where Celtic people arrived from Brittany in about 150 BC to work the Cornish tin mines. And after Caesar's conquest of Gaul, great numbers of refugees, notably from the maritime tribe of the Veneti, settled in Wessex. The political situation in Britain was extremely complex when the armies of the Emperor Claudius arrived to make the country a Roman province in AD 43, but we can imagine that it was equally so at almost any other point in the preceding three thousand years, if only we knew.

With this excessively brief summer of prehistory, let us turn again to the signatures which the diverse peoples have inscribed on the palimpsest of the British landscape. By a fortunate chance, many of the areas which were most densely populated in early times were later abandoned and neglected until the present century. The chief reason was the introduction of a heavy plough, ox-drawn and capable of tackling the heavy soils of the river valleys. It was apparently first brought to Britain by the Belgae, a Celtic tribe who appeared on the scene in the first century BC, but came into general use by the Saxons, after Roman civilization had virtually collapsed. The thin soils on the chalk downs and limestone hills relapsed into their primitive state of wiry grassland, slowly storing up fertility over the centuries until the time came for new techniques to make possible its exploitation at a time of need, in twentieth-century wars. In our own day the plough has destroyed many of the more fragile clues to ancient occupation. The downs are parcelled out into huge fields by barbed-wire fences, and luxuriant crops of barley grow where for over a thousand years sheep grazed. But sufficient areas of untouched downland remain as samples for us to study.

On many hill slopes we can see the outlines of ancient British fields. They are rectangular and enclosed by banks which make each field a kind of shallow terrace. Some of these banks measure three or four feet from top to bottom. Nearly all the fields are quite small, not more than an acre or so and often considerably less.

A variation on the theme of terraced fields is provided by the lynchets, which are terraces that follow the contours of hill slopes. The banks here are often even deeper and steeper, and parallel lynchets on either side of a narrow downland valley form a spectacular feature of some downland landscapes. They were almost certainly made after the introduction of the heavy plough with a mould-board designed to turn a furrow. But there is little to indicate the age of any particular lynchet, and while some, perhaps most, are pre-Roman, others may have been formed in mediaeval times.

The neglect of the high downs has preserved for us many of the ancient ridgeways trodden by men and pack animals for millennia. Some are long-distance routes, such as the Icknield Way which follows the line of the Chilterns from the Thames to East Anglia, the ridgeway which runs along the escarpment of the Berkshire Downs, overlooking the Vale of the White Horse, and the Pilgrims Way, of the North Downs; others are short stretches linking groups of fields with villages or with each other. On level ground the old tracks are marked only by shorter and greener turf, but in many instances on sloping terrain they have carved deep gullies to form sunken ways. In some places we can see a series of roughly parallel trenches, some of them twenty or more feet deep, on a hillside. In the course of centuries, as one track became too deep and difficult, the travellers simply made another a few yards away. The erosion of the track would be accelerated by the use of sledges, rather than wheeled traffic, and by rain. However, not all such tracks belong to prehistoric times. Parallel ditches of a similar type occur alongside Roman roads, and some continued to be used until quite recently.

On the subject of ancient trackways, Alfred Watkins in 1925 propounded an evocative theory in his book *The Old Straight Track* (reprinted in 1972). He visualized the countryside dissected by a network of lines drawn between sighting points such as cairns on hills, standing stones, earthworks, clumps of trees, tumuli and any other prominent feature which would lend itself to the purpose. It is along these lines, which he termed 'leys', that most ancient trackways are to be found, said Mr Watkins. From the point of view of the shaping of the countryside, the theory could have significance in that many points of future importance (the sites of villages and towns, for instance) could have had their origin as the intersection of prehistoric tracks and hence of leys. It is a fact that, in one of the districts which I know best, Stonehenge, Old Sarum, Salisbury Cathedral and the conspicuous hilltop earthwork of Clearbury Camp lie on a dead straight line, a ley which, extended northwards, also passes through a prehistoric site on Tan Hill.

An old tradition says that the site of Weyhill Fair in north Hampshire was at the point where the Tin Road from Cornwall crossed the Gold Road from Wales. Whether or not that is so, many of the older sheep-fairs were held on prehistoric sites, especially within the ramparts of old hilltop earthworks. Examples were Woodbury Hill Fair near Bere Regis, Dorset (immortalized by Thomas Hardy), Yarnbury Castle, in the centre of Salisbury Plain, and Westbury Hill Fair, held on the hill crest by the White Horse. That the holding of fairs on such sites represents a very ancient tradition dating back to the time when the earthworks were first constructed, perhaps for just that purpose, is by no means impossible.

It is tempting to regard the White Horse carved in the chalk on the steep escarpment of Westbury Hill, Wiltshire, as the work of prehistoric men, but the evidence is against it. The earliest documentary reference to the Horse is in 1742. The figure then in existence, however, was very much smaller than the present one (which was cut in 1778) and had certain features reminiscent of prehistoric art. But the 1742 report says that the carving had been "wrought within the memory of persons now living or but lately dead", and the generally accepted opinion is that it was fashioned very early in the eighteenth century.

Virtually all the other white horses of the chalk country (and there are more than a dozen of them) are of even later date, but the Uffington White Horse, which adorns the chalk ridge overlooking the Berkshire Vale of the White Horse, is a notable exception. It is undoubtedly prehistoric and may well have been the totem animal or god of the tribe inhabiting the Vale. If it were not known as a White Horse, no one would recognize a horse in the figure depicted. It looks more like a furtive alley-cat slinking away over the crest of the hill. But the surrealistic lines of which it is composed duplicated almost exactly those used to portray stylized horses on early Iron Age coins from Gaul.

Another hill figure of genuine antiquity is the Cerne Abbas Giant, on a hillside in West Dorset. He stands there, 180 feet high, naked and exposing his powerful virility to all, and brandishing a huge club with apparent menace. He is almost certainly a Celtic god, identified by some writers as Hercules or his Celtic counterpart. The Long Man of Wilmington, near Eastbourne, another giant figure, 231½ feet high, may also have a prehistoric origin as a Celtic deity, though other authorities have considered it to be the work of mediaeval monks.

Probably many other hillside figures once existed, but time can quickly obliterate them. Surviving examples need fairly frequent 'scouring', to clear away weeds and grass, re-face the bare patches with chalk, and accentuate the outlines, which are liable to slip downhill as the chalk is washed away by rain. In the 1960s traces of former figures, thought to have been Celtic gods and goddesses, are said to have been detected on the slopes of the Gogmagog Hills in Cambridgeshire.

Vaguely associated with the enigmatic hill figures is the alleged zodiac which Mrs Katherine Maltwood claimed to have discovered around Glastonbury in 1929. The figures of the zodiac are delineated by ancient tracks, dykes, hills, lanes and other features of the Somerset countryside. Some of them look convincing on a large-scale map, but others are obscure, and Mrs Maltwood has had to substitute a ship for the conventional sign of the Crab, and a dove for Libra. Archaeologists advise caution. But it is interesting that local inhabitants have a traditional rhyme about 'The Gurt Dog of Langport', the outline of whose figure they profess to see in certain features of the countryside (an area which overlaps or adjoins Mrs Maltwood's zodiac). The identification of the various features sound like punning attempts at humour, Head Drove representing the Dog's head, Earlake Moor its ear, and the hamlet of Wagg its tail! Nevertheless, the tradition is very old, antedating by perhaps centuries Mrs Maltwood's investigations.

A question which has puzzled many students is the whereabouts and nature of the dwellings of the men who erected Stonehenge, Avebury, Stanton Drew and the other megalithic monuments, who cut the hillside figures and were buried in the numerous barrows. How curious that we should have so much information about their graves and so little about their houses! That the builders of sophisticated edifices should have luxurious or even comfortable homes is by no means necessary, of course. It is not to be supposed that the artisans responsible for the great mediaeval cathedrals lived in anything but lowly huts; and the peasants who built the imposing Maya pyramids of Central America went home to flimsy, palm-thatched dwellings. Yet the Neolithic and Bronze Age inhabitants of Britain's chalk country need not have existed in such squalor as is sometimes imagined. For some reason, the possibilities of the local building material seem to have been ignored.

The preparation and use of chalk cob is now an obsolete craft, but only just, for my father, born in 1874, saw cottages being built of it. Chalk cob is the obvious building material for a countryside devoid of timber and stone. Rubbly chalk is mixed with water and a leavening of such materials as wheat chaff and animal hair, to give it consistency, and then trodden into a kind of paste. When a large heap of chalk had been piled up and water poured over it, a party of men tramped around on it, singing, it was said, the traditional Mudwaller's Song, the words and music of which have been lost but which was of undoubted antiquity. The 'stampers' wore either very heavy boots or fastened to their everyday footwear soles or pattens of iron, and while they worked, their comrades threw more water and more chalk on the now flattened heap.

When the gluey mixture was judged to be of the right consistency, it was picked up by means of flat-grained, three-tined prongs, like Neptune's trident or eel-spears, and thrown into position for a wall. Sometimes a flint foundation was provided; sometimes a shallow trench was filled with the cob. Little attempt was made to shape it at this stage; the material was simply thrown into a long heap and piled higher and higher until it began to collapse under its own weight. Operations were then suspended for a day or two, to allow the cob to dry, after which another layer was added. In cob walls which have lost their facing of plaster, it is easy to detect the layers or courses. Trimming to shape was carried out when the wall had reached the desired height. In Victorian times the tool used was a wooden saw. The surface was then plastered. Interior walls were constructed of hurdle-work plastered with lime and/or mud.

Such a wall is extraordinarily durable. During the Second World War bombs falling in a field adjacent to a cob-walled house in which I was then living failed to make any impression at all on it, though splitting other walls a quarter of a mile away. Houses with cob walls and thatched roofs are warm in winter and cool in summer and so are pleasant to live in. But for cob the secret of long life is 'to keep its head dry'. That is why cob walls around gardens or farmyards always have their tops protected by a narrow roof of either thatch or some modern building material, such as galvanized iron or asbestos. Once rain and frost begin to penetrate, the cob quickly disintegrates.

That, in my opinion, is why no traces of the dwellings of the megalithic builders have been found. Archaeologists have searched in vain for post holes and wall foundations, because there were none. Possibly, though, if they had looked for diffused areas of disintegrated cob, they might have found some clues; though perhaps not, for cob is easily carted away, to be used again or spread over the soil to help the lime content (a familiar agricultural practice). In another of my books (*The Folklore of Wiltshire*), I recall how a neighbour of mine, Ernest Judd, lived for ninety-nine years in a single-storeyed cob cottage in the village of Winterslow. "He died when the building was burned to the ground. Within a couple of weeks the site was levelled, the garden ploughed and incorporated in the adjacent field, and no one would ever have guessed that a building had ever stood there." So quickly and completely can a cob-walled building be eliminated.

The making of cob and the use of thatch are likely to have been among the earliest crafts developed by men, and there is nothing outrageous in the conjecture that the builders of Stonehenge were familiar with them.

Not many years ago, a site in the south-eastern corner of Salisbury Plain was investigated and proved to be the burial-ground of villagers who had lived in the area towards the end of the Roman era, coins of the early fourth century AD being found in some of the graves. These people were obviously poor but independent peasants, and still pagan, for no suggestion of Christianity was found. The burials were grouped around a central pit, of unknown depth but filled nearly to the top with a kind of creamy-brown pasty material, now stone-hard. The pit remained unexcavated and the material unidentified, but, having seen similar stuff before, I think I could recognize it. It was disintegrated cob. I would surmise that the burials (some cremations and some inhumations) had been made in a cob-walled building, probably thatched and erected over this pit. In sound Celtic tradition, the pit would have been considered an entrance to the Underworld. In due course, the walls had collapsed into the pit and there solidified into an amorphous mass.

Returning from this digression, we may perhaps legitimately summarize by suggesting that, when we find chalk cob in the chalk country or mud cob in Devon and elsewhere, we may be looking at examples of a craft (though not, of course, at the actual edifices) that originated four or five thousand years ago.

Flints, on which the Stone Age culture was based, are, of course, found in chalk measures. Layers of them may be seen in exposed chalk faces. In search of the best, early men sank shafts as deep as twenty or thirty feet, shaping a labyrinth of galleries at the bottom, when they had reached the very hard, black, 'floorstone' flint. One of the best-known flint-mines is at Grime's Graves, near Thetford, in Norfolk, where, somewhat surprisingly, the miners had to dig through about ten feet of silt, sand and boulder clay before they reached the chalk. The excavations are open to the public and offer such interesting illustrations of life in those far-off days as finger-prints on the handles of antler picks and the soot marks cast by lamps on the gallery ceilings. Altogether there are seven to eight hundred pits in the Grime's Graves area, and the official handbook for the site surmises that if one assumes a total work-force of nine persons, sinking on average three pits a year, the mines would have been worked for less than three centuries. It seems that the major exploitation of the site ended in about 1900 BC. Incidentally, nearby at Brandon the prehistoric craft of flint-knapping still survives, though now confined, I believe, to producing flints for flintlock guns.

The South Downs near Worthing have another concentration of flint-mines, and there is an important one at Easton Down, on the Hampshire-Wiltshire border (though this last is not open to the public). No doubt many others remain to be discovered. As the miners exhausted a mine, they would throw the accumulated chalk and rubble into it; this, in time, would settle, leaving a shallow pit, with perhaps a flanking group of low mounds, as surface indications.

In other parts of Britain, other types of stone were quarried. A grey-green stone found in the Lake District was much in demand for axe-heads, examples of which have been mapped from all over the country. The fact that the blue stones of the Prescelly Mountains of Pembrokeshire were laboriously conveyed to Stonehenge is an indication of the high value placed on stones from this source. Doubtless religion was involved, but axes and other tools of the same stone (alternatively known as spotted dolerite or preselite) have occurred in other parts of Britain.

Towards the end of the Neolithic Age, mining of other rocks began. The techniques of smelting ore and of mixing ninety per cent of copper with ten per cent of tin to form bronze were evolved in the Near East but were later widely practised in Britain. Early copper-mines have been located at several sites in Scotland, Ireland and Wales, all in use in the Bronze Age.

Tin-mines were confined to Cornwall, Cornish tin being known and prized in the Mediterranean world at a quite early date. Gold was at first obtained by the washing of gravels in river-beds, notably in Ireland and Scotland. Mining gold probably began in the Iron Age in Wales, one of the ancient sites (near Dolgelly, Merionethshire) being still worked occasionally. Iron workings belong, of course, to the Iron Age. In Britain iron occurs in several ores, some of the earliest of which to be worked are in districts not now associated with iron mining, such as Dartmoor, Cornwall, the Mendips and central Wiltshire. The iron deposits of the Weald began to be exploited in the centuries immediately preceding the coming of the Romans, as men started to penetrate the dense, tangled forest. At the same period some lead was mined in the Mendips and in Yorkshire.

In stone districts, stones lying about on the surface or easily obtainable from outcrops were doubtless used for a variety of purposes. As far back as the Neolithic era chambered tombs were being constructed of stones fitted together without mortar, and, of course, the trilithons of Stonehenge itself have their lintels fitted over tenons on the supporting uprights, without the aid of mortar. Employing stones, which needed to be moved from the fields anyway, for making the boundary walls of enclosures, would seem to be an obvious exercise, and there can be little doubt that long before Roman times Britons were expert at erecting drystone walls. The art of making the field walls which are so much a feature of the landscape in the highland half of Britain was thus perfected in prehistoric times, and it is at least possible that some of the walls have survived for two thousand years or more, for boundary walls tend to be kept in repair as long as they serve a useful purpose and are seldom moved.

In districts devoid of stone, other ways of marking boundaries and preventing cattle and sheep from straying had to be devised. One of the most effective was and is the construction of live hedges. That a barrier of dead thorn bushes was a useful deterrent both to wandering animals and to raiders must have occurred to prehistoric man at an early date; it is so obvious. What needed much more ingenuity was the development of the art of weaving a hedge from growing wood. The stems and trunks of bushes are slashed half through just above ground level, so that the bushes may be bent over at an oblique angle and woven around upright stakes hammered into the ground at short intervals. The effect, wrote Julius Caesar, who encountered the device employed as a military defence in his campaign against the Belgae in north-eastern Gaul, was to create a barrier "through which it was impossible to see, let alone to penetrate". As Caesar was meeting this device for the first time, it may be assumed that it was invented or perfected by the Belgae or their fellow Celts. We can therefore regard the hedge as a comparatively new feature of Iron Age Britain, which, of course, gives the hedges still neatly 'laid' by experts in many an English shire a venerable ancestry.

The art or craft of weaving withies, hazel rods and other supple twigs and brushwood is even more ancient. Hurdle-work is visible in certain long barrows dating from very early in the Neolithic period. Stone Age men must have been adept at weaving ropes to bind their stone axe-heads to the hafts; and it is thought that they descended into their flint-mines by means of rope ladders. In Ulster, at the point where the River Bann emerges from Lough Neagh, archaeologists have discovered the remains of wicker weirs, very similar to those still used by local fishermen. Radio-carbon dating has shown that they were in use in about 6,000 BC. Very much later, there are several records in literature of the wickerwork figures in which the Celtic Druids burned sacrificial victims. Storage pits for grain, which are numerous on the downs of Wessex and which are mostly of Iron Age date, are lined with basketwork. In general, of course, most examples of the skill of prehistoric men in this direction have perished, but when we see a modern basket-maker or hurdle-maker at work, it is interesting to reflect that he is exercising a skill that has been known for many thousands of years.

Basket-weaving naturally flourishes where willow is most plentiful, and it is not surprising therefore to find it in the Somerset lowlands. What is, perhaps, a little unexpected is to find people living on permanent sites in the marshes in prehistoric times. Three or four miles north-west of Glastonbury was a largish lake, Meare Pool, the last sections of which were drained in 1712. In it were two villages, the sites of which have been excavated, that were evidently occupied from about 250 BC to AD 50. They were constructed on man-made islands, the foundations of which were massive timbers driven into the bottom of the lake. One of them covered an area of three acres and contained sixty-five clay and wattle huts. They were connected with the shores of the lake by causeways, each with a twelve-foot gap spanned by a drawbridge. The villagers grazed their flocks and herds on the mainland and had cultivated fields there, but in time of danger they could retreat to what must have been an almost impregnable stronghold.

Nothing similar has so far been found in the Fens of eastern England, but there are traces of artificial waterways which seem to pre-date the Roman era.

Superficially, the impact of religion on the landscape might seem to be slight, but in reality it is quite profound. After all, it is more than likely that the builders of Stonehenge, Avebury and the other major megalithic monuments were inspired by religion, and burials throughout prehistory were evidently made in the expectation of an after-life. The survival of these monuments for so many centuries is little short of miraculous. Beyond doubt there were once many more, some destroyed within recent times (as at Tisbury, Wiltshire, where in the eighteenth century a local landowner carted the huge stones of an Avebury-like monument for several miles across country and used them to make an ornamental grotto). Seventeenth- and eighteenth-century documents describe methods for splitting the great stones, by the use of fire and water, into fragments of a suitable size for building material. There is every likelihood that many of our churches stand on sites formerly sacred to older religions and contain in their walls stones from earlier pagan shrines. The greater part of the village of Avebury lies within the Neolithic stone circle; the ruined church of Knowlton, in Dorset, is in the centre of a prehistoric earthwork; and numerous similar examples could be cited.

We know little about religious thought in Britain in the BC millennia, at least until the arrival of the Celts. Then the accounts by Roman authors of the Celtic priesthood, the Druids, throw some light on the subject, though at best the Romans were both biased and incompletely informed.

Whether the Celtic religion in any way resembled creeds that had formerly held sway, we cannot say. In spite of the ceremonies of the modern Order of Druids (founded in AD 1781), there is no certain connection between the Celtic Druids and Stonehenge, and some leading authorities pour scorn on the idea that any ever existed, though there must be just the possibility that Druids appropriated the stones for their own rituals.

But while we cannot unravel which elements are Celtic and which pre-Celtic, we do possess a mass of pagan survivals, mostly under a Christian camouflage. It seems that prehistoric Britain was nearly as thickly populated by numinous and elusive beings as by visible humans. Every river and pool, every standing stone and spring, many hills and many trees, had their resident spirit or nymph. The unseen realm of 'fairyland' existed side by side with the material world, and access could be obtained to it through enchanted hills and secret passages. The Celts in particular were so sure of another life that they would contract to repay a debt in the next world.

The year was divided into four quarters, with quarter days on 1st (or 2nd) February, known as Imbolc; May Day, or Beltane; Lugnasad, in early August; and Samhain, All Saints' Day. It was a pastoral calendar, based on sheep and cattle husbandry rather than on arable farming. And what happened to the quarter days is typical of the transformation of all the old pagan festivals. For Imbolc became Candlemas; May Day, Whitsuntide; Lugnasad, Lammas-tide; and Samhain, when the veil between the two worlds wore extremely thin, allowing spirits to wander at will over the earth, became All Saints' Day, though with the emphasis on the Eve of that festival – Hallowe'en. All are examples of the policy of the early Christian Church to appropriate and Christianize traditions which it was powerless to suppress. In due course it adopted the same policy towards the Anglo-Saxon and Norse religions.

So, when Morris dancers parade and mummers perform their Christmas drama, and 5th November bonfires blaze, and apple trees are wassailed, and corn dollies adorn harvest-home suppers, we see re-enacted ceremonies the origins of which lie far back in the mists of prehistory. And, if it is objected that these festivals have little to do with the *shape* of the countryside, it is relevant to point out that in many instances they are associated with places. Bonfires are built on certain hills each autumn. The wells or springs that are dressed with flowers in May were doubtless sacred fountains long ago. Sacred trees were useful landmarks and as such often became nodal points of boundaries which are still valid today. Sometimes the traditional site of a dance or a fair suggests an ancient shrine or holy place. For instance, an ancient record refers to mediaeval dancers wearing antlers performing their dance on Ludgate Hill, by St Paul's Cathedral – an indication, surely, that the site was once a sacred eminence where horned dancers, like those of Abbots Bromley, in Staffordshire, participated in a religious ceremony.

As we emerge, therefore, from the long shadows of prehistory, we survey a countryside altered in many respects from its primaeval state. The open country, notably the downs and the moors of the west, is quite thickly populated and is alive with human voices. Peasants are cultivating the upland fields; aristocrats clatter about in two-wheeled chariots and delight in daring displays of horsemanship; fishermen float on estuaries in beetle-like coracles, netting salmon; priests officiate over elaborate ceremonies in mysterious groves; travelling smiths, tinkers and pedlars tramp the grassy ridgeways. Many a hilltop is crowned by formidable ramparts, not soothingly green as now but glaring white with newly excavated chalk. Standing stones mark the sites of future churches and hence of villages and towns. Mines are operating in the west and north, and stone quarries are gashing hillsides. Little ports are crowded with ships, for voyages across the Channel and even across the North Sea and the Bay of Biscay are commonplace. Man is beginning to shape his environment to his own needs.

Yet still more than half of the country is much as ever it was – gloomy forests into which men, except for outlaws and brigands, seldom venture. The conquest of the forest must await another age. Apart from the few instances already mentioned, too, the vast areas of marsh and fen are likewise out of bounds to most of the human race. And a deterioration of climate in the last millennium BC has resulted in the formation of extensive peat bogs, which are inhospitable places for men.

3

The Roman Legacy

The Roman drove his metalled way
O'er hill and valley in his day.
The skilful Roman engineer
Essayed a steady course to steer.

Swift, stream-lined cars appreciate
The Roman's rigid estimate
And bound, like gimmers newly shorn,
Over the downs by Nadderbourne.

The great highways are indeed the most conspicuous legacy bequeathed to us by the Romans. After seventeen or eighteen hundred years, long sections of Watling Street, Ermine Street, the Fosse Way and many other roads with which the Roman army confined Britain in a strategic network still do service as trunk roads. They have been surpassed though not superseded only by the railways in the nineteenth century and the motorways constructed during the past two decades.

The Roman road system was essentially military. The major highways were laid down piecemeal, in accordance with military requirements, in the years following the Conquest; minor roads came later, in more settled times.

After Julius Caesar's reconnaissance in 54 BC, Britain continued to remain outside the Roman Empire for more than ninety years, though probably with increasing apprehension. Four legions were despatched across the Channel in AD 43 by the Emperor Claudius to effect the subjugation of the Britons. It is generally assumed that they landed in Kent, fought a battle with the British forces at the crossing of the Medway and then advanced to London or somewhere in the vicinity of where London would later stand. There they waited for Claudius himself to arrive from Rome, to deliver the *coup de grâce.* The objective was Camulodunum (Colchester), the capital or chief settlement of the king Cunobelinus, who governed that part of Britain. Claudius remained in the country just sixteen days, being chiefly occupied with receiving the submission of crestfallen tribesmen. He then returned to Rome to celebrate a triumph, leaving his generals to complete the Conquest.

The first major frontier established by the Romans in Britain was along the line of the Fosse Way, anchored to Gloucester (Glevum) in the south-west and Lincoln (Lindum) in the north-east. Once the entire country to the south-east of this line had been thoroughly absorbed into the Roman system, the advance began a second phase. A campaign against the Brigantes of northern England was followed by the establishment of York (Eboracum) as a major base, while on the other side of the Pennines, Chester was founded as a permanent fortress to control the crossing of the River Dee and as a base for a legionary garrison keeping an eye on North Wales.

Arriving as Governor of Britain in AD 78, Agricola immediately set about organizing a series of vigorous campaigns which resulted in the completion of the conquest of North Wales and then took Roman armies into the heart of the Scottish Highlands. There, at a place recorded as Mons Graupius, the identity of which is now unknown, the climactic battle of the British war was fought, ending in an overwhelming victory for the Romans. To complete the triumph, a Roman fleet navigated around the entire coast of Scotland. From the first landing in Kent, the Conquest had taken forty-one years.

Thereafter Britain was a province of the Roman Empire for about three centuries, with the exclusion of Scotland which was abandoned to native tribes. The southern and eastern parts of the island were thoroughly Romanized, the local aristocracy receiving a Roman education, adopting Roman manners and considering themselves Romans. There was, in fact, no differentiation made between the numerous races within the Empire. A Syrian or an Egyptian might freely settle in Britain, a Briton in Asia Minor or North Africa. That, in the Dark Ages which followed the decline of the Empire, Britain reverted to a predominantly Celtic culture, is, in a way, surprising. Three hundred years is a substantial slice of time for a civilization to leave its imprint on a countryside. However, the Roman contribution is greater than we sometimes imagine.

The Conquest completed, the great roads began to develop their secondary function, of carrying trade and other civilian traffic. The major highways were linked by lesser ones, and all were thronged with people and vehicles. They served to link the towns which were springing up in the shelter of the Roman peace, perhaps for the first time in Britain.

Whether any pre-Roman settlements in Britain should be considered true towns is a matter of some controversy. The tribes which divided the country between them before the Conquest seem to have had 'capitals', in the form of hill fortifications, but it seems likely that the huts within the earthworks were mere haphazard conglomerations. In the pacification that followed the military campaigns, the general policy of the Roman governors was to move the British population out of the hill-forts into a town, laid out according to Roman patterns, on lower ground. Thus, the survivors from the sack of Maiden Castle moved down to an open site nearby and there built the Romano-British town of Durnovaria (modern Dorchester). The old hill-fort of Bagendon, which was the headquarters of the tribe of the Dobunni, seems to have been entirely abandoned in favour of the lowland settlement of Corinium (afterwards Cirencester). In Shropshire the movement was evidently downhill from The Wrekin to Uriconium (Wroxeter).

In addition to encouraging or forcing this development, the Romans deliberately planted two other kinds of towns. One was, of course, the military fortress, around which in due course a town developed. The other was the establishment of *coloniae*, settlements of retired soldiers. Often the two types merged, a favourite site for a *colonia* being in the immediate vicinity of a garrison town.

The earliest of the *coloniae* in Britain was Camulodunum (Colchester), the 'capital' of Cunobelinus, the British king of those parts. A space of over a hundred acres on the south bank of the River Colne was laid out into neat, rectangular chequers. One chequer was devoted to a *forum*, or market, another to a magnificent temple in white stone dedicated (probably) to the Emperor Claudius. The town was populated by, in addition to officials and administrators, retired veterans from two of the legions employed in the invasion. It seems that they were provided with lands dispossessed, with some harshness, from the local British inhabitants. Whether any of the latter settled within the confines of the new *colonia*, and if so on what terms, is not known. The town was founded, or at least the temple was erected, in the year AD 50, when it seemed that the south of Britain was finally pacified, for no fortifications or even a defensive wall were erected. Eleven years later the revolt of Boudicca caught the inhabitants of the new township completely unprepared, and all perished in a holocaust of savagery and cruelty. In due course, the town was rebuilt, and several modern buildings have been found to have exactly the same foundations as their Roman predecessors.

Lindum (Lincoln) and Glevum (Gloucester) were also established as *coloniae* at an early date, and Eboracum (York) later, probably about the beginning of the third century AD. The other principal towns of Roman Britain were as follows:

Londinium (London) probably existed in some form in pre-Roman times but assumed great importance in Roman Britain through the development of trade with the Continent. It has been suggested that Londinium owed its initial prosperity to the very fact that it was not a *colonia* and so, having no particular status, was allowed to develop its trade freely. Later in the Roman era it became the most important town in the province of Britannia Prima and the seat of the administration.

Durovernum (Canterbury) – The site of Canterbury was occupied, though to what extent is unknown, in pre-Roman times. Roman Canterbury covered about 120 acres and was one of the first towns to be regarded as a provincial or tribal capital. It was the centre of a countryside which was most completely Romanized and enjoyed considerable trade with the Continent.

Caesaromagus (Chelmsford) – This was the chief town in the territory of the Trinovantes tribe. It has been suggested that the town was created as compensation for land sequestrated to form the *colonia* of Camulodunum. The subsequent involvement of the Trinovantes with Queen Boudicca's rebellion may have had a bearing on the failure of

Caesaromagus to develop like other towns founded about the same time.

Verulamium (St Albans) – In pre-Roman times this Belgic settlement was one of the capitals of the tribe of the Catuvellauni. It was re-planned by the Romans and retained its status as a tribal capital, achieving considerable prosperity. It lies on the great highway of Watling Street.

Calleva Atrebatum (Silchester) – The capital of the tribe of the Atrebates, Silchester, in the forest country of northern Hampshire, is one of the few important Roman towns which has not survived to the present. In consequence, a more complete excavation than in most other instances has been possible. Silchester seems to have been a pleasant, modest-sized country town, on the lines of a garden city, which enjoyed a reasonable prosperity until well into the fifth century.

Venta Belgarum (Winchester) – At the time of the Conquest, the present site of Winchester was inhabited and protected by an earthwork. It later became the capital of an administrative unit, *civitas Belgarum*, created by the Romans out of old tribal territories. It seems to have had a considerable population.

Noviomagus Regnensium (Chichester) – This may have been the capital of the Regnensis, a tribe which sided with the Romans at the time of the invasion and was consequently well treated, or it may have been planned after the Conquest, to replace an earlier administrative centre, possibly at Selsey. Nearby, at Fishbourne, a magnificent palace has been partially excavated.

Corinium (Cirencester) – The Romano-British town, capital of the tribe of the Dobunni, which superseded the hill-top settlement of Bagendon nearby. It seems to have achieved considerable prosperity and to have retained its importance until well into the sixth century.

Durnovaria (Dorchester) developed as one of the capitals of the canton of the Durotriges after the taking of Maiden Castle in an early phase of the Conquest. There is evidence of considerable industrial activity, and in the later years of the Roman era the town seems to have been an important centre of Christianity.

Isca Dumnoniorum (Exeter) – The probability is that the Romans found no centralized control and no tribal 'capitals' in the domains of the Dumnonii, who occupied the Devon-Cornwall peninsula and that therefore it was they who founded Exeter on what seemed to be the most suitable site. In Roman times it seems to have been an outpost of urban civilization in a territory inhabited by rural folk who preferred their old ways.

Durotrigum Lindinensis (Ilchester) – A secondary tribal capital of the Durotriges, probably developed for political reasons, to split into half a troublesome tribe. It occupies a strategic site, where the Fosse Way crosses the River Yeo at a point below which the river expands into what were then impassable marshlands.

Isca Silurum (Caerleon) – This was a military fortress, on the lines of Lindum and Glevum, built to keep the warlike Silures tribe of South Wales in check.

Venta Silurum (Caerwent) – After the Conquest this town developed as the tribal centre of the Silures. It seems to have enjoyed a modest prosperity.

Moridunum Demetarum (Carmarthen) – After the conquest of Wales this fort was constructed to keep an eye on the Demetae tribe, who occupied much of modern Carmarthenshire and Pembrokeshire. In default of any other settlements worthy of the name of a town, it apparently developed as a tribal capital.

Glevum (Gloucester) – A strong *colonia* for retired legionaries was planted at a quite early date on the edge of this important military fortress.

Ratae Coritanorum (Leicester) – The indications are that the Coritani, a tribe which occupied a large zone of central England before the Conquest, were not very wealthy or important. Ratae, however, not far from the intersection of the Fosse Way and Watling Street, had considerable strategic significance, and in the later Roman period the town seems to have been busy and prosperous.

Virconium Cornoviorum (Wroxeter) – No towns seem to have existed in the territory of the Cornovii (Shropshire and the adjacent region) before the Roman era, and Virconium (sometimes spelt Uriconium) was first established as a military fort. It later became one of the largest towns in Britain, at least in area, for it extended over 180 acres, and there is some evidence that it was prosperous to match.

Venta Icenorum (Caistor-by-Norwich) – This town seems to

have been established as an administrative centre for what was left of the tribe of the Iceni after the rebellion of Boudicca in AD 61. It fell early to Anglo-Saxon invaders.

Lindum (Lincoln) – As with Gloucester, a strong *colonia* of retired legionaries was established around the great fort built early in the period of the Conquest. The town remained one of the most important in Britain throughout the Roman era.

Petuaria (Brough-on-Humber) – Somewhere on the north bank of the Humber, in the vicinity of Brough and North Ferriby, an important fort, naval base and provincial capital, associated with the tribe of the Parisi, flourished in Roman times, but the exact site is uncertain.

Colonia Eboracensium (York) – York seems to have been founded as a military base for the subjugation of Brigantia, the kingdom of the powerful northern tribes, the Brigantes, in AD 71. Later a *colonia* of veterans was established there. The town became the administrative capital of Britannia Inferior, the northern province of Britain, and the site of an imperial palace.

Isurium Brigantum (Aldborough) – An important fort on the road north from York, around which a thriving trading town had a history for a century or two.

Deva (Chester) – An important fortress which served the purpose not only of a base against formidable tribes in north Wales but also of cutting contact between those tribes and the troublesome nation of the Brigantes.

Luguvalium (Carlisle) – This town probably began its career as a fortress near the western end of Hadrian's Wall but afterwards became the administrative centre of a canton carved out of the north-western sector of Brigantian territory.

Aquae Sulis (Bath) holds an anomalous position among Romano-British towns, in that it owes nothing to military considerations, nor was it an administrative centre. It grew up around the hot springs which bubble, at a temperature of 120°F, out of the rocks and were reputed to have curative powers. The masonry with which the Romans penned and utilized the waters is still largely intact and is annually inspected by crowds of tourists.

Besides these major centres, Roman Britain was studded with numerous minor towns and forts. The suffixes or prefixes 'caster', 'cester', 'chester', 'xeter', 'caer' and the like, derived from the Latin *castra* – a camp – on many present-day towns and villages reveal their Roman origin. Some, such as Caistor-on-the-Wolds, Dorchester-on-Thames, Irchester, Ancaster, Grantchester, Ribchester and Woodchester, have remained relatively small and unimportant places, while others, such as Manchester, Doncaster, Chester itself, Rochester, Leicester, Gloucester and Exeter, have grown into major cities.

The idea that the early Anglo-Saxon invaders had a superstitious dread of stone houses and gave them a wide berth is widely accepted, and to a large extent it may be true. But the peoples who came flocking in after the collapse of the military might of the Empire were a heterogeneous lot, doubtless including renegades and escaped slaves and criminals, as well as tribesmen from Scotland and Ireland and the far side of the North Sea, and not all would have avoided the ruins of the towns. In many instances, there seems to have been a tenuous continuity of occupation. In others, after a brief hiatus, the old sites began to be reoccupied.

It is a tribute to the Roman eye for strategic positions that, when the time came for urban life to be revived, in so many instances no better sites could be found than those established by the Romans. Of the primitive and largely untamed canvas of Britain, Rome imposed her typical pattern of nucleated cities linked by straight roads, much of which has survived to this day. The reason for its survival is that it could hardly be bettered.

From the viewpoint of our theme, the shaping of the countryside, therefore, we may claim that one effect of the Roman presence was to remove certain territory permanently from the countryside. From the city of London and the central areas of Lincoln, York, Exeter, Gloucester and other towns, forests, meadows, ploughlands and pastures were irretrievably banished.

With these alien islets of urbanization we have little concern, except in that they were the embryos from which would grow monstrous entities which would seize and pollute vast areas of countryside. It is interesting to reflect, however, that they were indeed alien from their very inception. The Roman towns were constructed to a standard pattern which had been perfected in other parts of the Empire. Each had its *forum*, baths, law courts and streets laid out in formal, chequer-board pattern; and most had aqueducts and main sewers. For citizens wealthy and secure enough to take advantage of these amenities, life was gracious and pleasant. But transplanting a Mediterranean town-plan to our austere northern land was not entirely successful, and although some of the British aristocracy were content to become Romanized and to live in the new towns, others were not. Some of the Roman foundations, such as Petuaria, apparently faltered and withered even before the legions departed.

Indeed, from the end of the third century onwards, city life in Britain was on the decline. One reason was the flight of the wealthier citizens to their country estates, in an attempt to avoid the taxman. They had made their pile, and all they wanted was to be left in peace. As they represented the chief spending-power in Britain, their exodus from the towns had a marked effect on trade.

But Britain had always been essentially rural. Estimates of the population of Britain during the Roman era range from about half a million to approaching two million. Of these at least two-thirds were working-class people, mostly peasants. Agriculture was far and away the main industry of the province, and large quantities of corn were regularly exported (though these were not necessarily surplus to the needs of the peasants, who probably could with advantage have used them themselves). Some mining was carried on. Manufactures, such as pottery and metalware, for the most part served local needs only. Prominent among exports were hunting-dogs and slaves.

The country estates to which the Romano-British retreated were great farms grouped around a country house known as a villa. It resembled the country houses of the eighteenth century, and life for the owners and their families must have been much the same as that of their eighteenth-century counterparts. The estate would employ an ample staff of retainers (though in the case of the Roman unit, slaves would feature prominently) and would supply most of the household's ordinary needs. Doubtless time would be passed in hunting and other rural pursuits, including a round of social visits.

The villas, of which more than five hundred have been mapped and investigated, were situated on the most attractive sites available. Southward-facing parkland sloping down to a stream, flanked by forests and with a mild southern climate was typical of the type of country favoured. The heavy plough, introduced into southern Britain in the century before the Conquest, was sufficiently widely known and used to enable the stiffer but more fertile soils of the lowlands to be utilized, while the clearance of areas of forest presented no problem to Roman organization.

Near my birthplace in south-eastern Wiltshire at least three villas have been discovered and others suspected. All are in fertile, lowland country and occupy some of the best sites in the district. The Roman highway from Venta Belgarum (Winchester) to Sorbiodunum (Salisbury) slashes across the high downs to the north, where in Roman times the native population still lived. Parts of one of their villages, still populated late in the fourth century AD, have been excavated. The folk who lived there were poor peasants but independent, for they had hobnailed boots and were buried in them and could afford to have a coin placed in their mouths, to pay the ferryman of the underworld. But their coffins were fastened with the minimum of nails (six), and some bodies were buried without coffins. Some had evidently been executed. The outlines of the rectangular fields which they cultivated are still visible on the upper slopes of the downs, and the hillsides are carved with their field tracks.

It is evident from this and from other similar arrangements elsewhere that the two sets of rural economies existed side by side. In the rich valley, the wealthy Romano-British aristocrat, with his centrally-heated villa, his riding-stables, battalion of servants and everything that went to compose a gracious and luxurious standard of living. On the hills, within two or three miles, the poverty-stricken native village where peasants still scratched the thin downland soil with light ploughs and bush-harrows to produce meagre crops. Yet it was on these peasants that the brunt of taxation fell, especially in southern Britain and wherever initial opposition to the Conquest had been strong. Historians have calculated that in Cranborne Chase, Dorset, as much as three-fifths of the annual produce was taken in taxes, as against one-tenth or one-twelfth which was more usual. The area in which this heavy imposition applied has since been extended by later excavations to much of Dorset, Wiltshire and eastern Hampshire. Over in the eastern counties, the Iceni, after their rebellion, were forced to labour under terms which were probably even less favourable. It seems evident that little or no attempt was made to introduce better methods of husbandry, to impose new systems of agriculture or land tenure on the peasants, or indeed to interfere with their lives in any way. So long, and it was often a savage proviso, as they paid their dues, they were allowed to live or die as they pleased.

Those dues included not only cash payments and quotas of grain and other produce but unpaid service on certain public works, notably roads. The roads were, of course, major engineering construction. They were of varying width, sometimes as much as eighty to ninety feet, with a deep ditch on either side and usually had an excavated bed on which were rammed foundations of stones, flints, gravel or other material, even timber in wooded districts. Sometimes the surface was paved, and often when passing through valleys the road was raised many feet high to form a causeway. Work on road maintenance or construction was probably under the supervision of Roman officials, who saw to it that the peasants did not shirk their obligations. Changing-stations for horses were provided at intervals of about twelve miles, and these too had to be supplied by the local inhabitants. Horses could be requisitioned if not readily forthcoming.

It is not really surprising that the Roman roads have endured the test of the centuries better than have the contemporary villas. The roads had a continuing value to successive waves of invaders and settlers, whereas the villas, once vacated, quickly relapsed into useless ruins. The common place-name 'Cold Harbour' is thought to indicate the site of a former Roman villa, where, in the Dark Ages, a benighted traveller could find lodging, albeit decidedly cold and uncomfortable. As already noted, the villas were built mostly on fertile lowland soil, which implies land reclaimed from forest, so when they were abandoned, the forest naturally returned. Many villa sites are still covered by dense woodland.

Two other important features of the Roman era remain to be noticed. The first is Hadrian's Wall, the second, the draining of some of the Fen country.

The Wall was one of the basic facts of life for the inhabitants of Roman Britain. After Agricola's campaign in Scotland, culminating in the battle of Mons Graupius, the Roman army occupied the whole of lowland Scotland and built a line of forts at the entrances to the Highland passes. These were manned for nearly thirty years, until, about the year AD 100, the garrisons had to be withdrawn for service elsewhere in the Empire. In the period AD 117–119 a major rising appears to have occurred in the North, and the Ninth Legion, formerly stationed at York, disappears from history in what must have been a disaster of the first magnitude.

It was followed by a visit of the highly capable Emperor Hadrian in AD 122, who initiated the building of the wall which bears his name. The site chosen was the narrowest part of the northern peninsula, between the Solway and the Tyne. There the Roman engineers constructed a wall eight to ten feet thick and seventy-three miles long. At intervals were seventeen major forts, about eighty castles and some 160 signal towers. On the north side, the wall was protected by a thirty-foot ditch. The eastern section had a stone wall sixteen feet high on the north side, offering protection to sentries patrolling along a broad walk on top of the rampart. The western section was somewhat lower and constructed largely of turf. A secondary ditch on the south side of the wall seems to have been designed against a possible attack from the rear. Some eight to ten thousand troops garrisoned the Wall on a more or less permanent basis. Farther to the west, a series of forts along both the Cumbrian and the Galloway shores of the Solway afforded flanking protection.

The Wall was thus, with the camp-followers and ancillaries of the garrison, one of the major centres of population in Roman Britain. In effect, it was one vast, elongated city. Some of the fortresses were designed to hold a thousand infantry, and each soon acquired a satellite village. Each mile-tower was provisioned with sufficient food to last for a year, and at Corbridge, on the Tyne, an enormous base-camp was established. There were both at Corbridge and on the Wall bath-houses, private houses, temples, shrines, markets and all the other appurtenances of a busy town. Much of the Wall still survives and is one of the most impressive ancient monuments in Britain.

The Wall must not be thought of as a rigid frontier line, like the Berlin Wall of modern times. Rather, it was a base for military operations. In times of peace, tribesmen, who were much the same on either side of the Wall, passed with relative freedom and traded with the garrison. Nor did the Roman army sit supinely behind their fortifications, allowing the enemy to come to them. Patrols and expeditions deep into the north were frequent.

About twenty years after the building of Hadrian's Wall, it was felt that another wall in an advanced position would be helpful, so, in the reign of Antoninus Pius, the Antonine Wall was built across the isthmus between the Firth of Forth and the Firth of Clyde. Following the line of a series of forts erected by Agricola, this Wall was largely of turf but with very steep slopes on either side and protected by deep ditches before and behind. The forts, though smaller, were more closely spaced and were designed as bases for further aggression as much as for defence. New roads, protected by a series of forts, linked Hadrian's Wall with the advanced positions on the Antonine.

In spite of all this, the period AD 155 to 158 saw unrest flaring into revolt in the North. The situation was dealt with in the usual ruthless Roman manner, but in 186 it was thought expedient to withdraw from the Antonine Wall and back to Hadrian's Wall. Unfortunately, that complex had been neglected in favour of the northern line, with the result that the discontented tribesmen were able to penetrate it at will for a time and to do enormous damage. When peace was eventually restored in the time of the Emperor Severus, who came to Britain in 208 and conducted a campaign in the North, much of Hadrian's Wall was in need of complete rebuilding. However, from that time onwards for a hundred years, it kept the North in comparative peace. So long as it was adequately garrisoned, it was virtually invulnerable. During those hundred years the inhabitants of southern Britain normally slept securely in their beds, aware that the northern defences provided a safeguard against attack from the most dangerous quarter. Not that they were allowed to forget entirely what was involved in their security. Two inscriptions on Hadrian's Wall testify to the work done by a detachment from Lindinis (Ilchester, in Somerset). It seems likely that the tribal authorities of those parts (doubtless wealthy landowners by this date) were required to supply a working-party. We may imagine a contingent of Somerset lads, probably slaves, marching the length of Britain along the Roman roads, their spades and pickaxes in their hands.

Among the reasons for the Roman invasion in the first place was the desire to exploit still further the agricultural potential of Britain. Considerable quantities of grain already found their way from Britain to Rome, and it was rightly argued that the quota might well be increased. In particular, the Romans had had much experience in the draining and reclamation of marshlands, of which vast areas were known to exist in eastern Britain. One of the early enterprises undertaken after the Conquest, therefore, was the taming of large areas of the Fens. Very ambitious drainage schemes, unmatched till the seventeenth century, were undertaken. Great canals, such as the Car Dyke in Cambridgeshire and Lincolnshire, which served the purposes of both drainage and transport, were dug and the adjacent land reclaimed for agriculture. Much of the work was apparently done, under terms of humiliating servitude, by the survivors of the Iceni, whose ancestral lands the Fens conveniently adjoin. Other major canals were constructed, making it possible to travel by inland waterways from the Fens to York. Considerable areas of former Fenland were thus made available for corn-growing, but apparently, once the preliminary work was done, native peasants were left to use it according to their traditional methods of husbandry, though with tax-collectors on their tails. The great reclamation works could have brought little joy to the farmers thus accommodated.

A bird's-eye view of Britain towards the end of the Roman era would reveal a countryside not unlike that of the early eighteenth century. In fact, from the height of Roman civilization to the beginning of the Industrial Revolution would have been a very short step. It could have been accomplished in fifty years instead of thirteen hundred.

We would see well-organized country estates, with comfortable and often luxurious mansions, broad rectangular fields, well-kept fences, sleek cattle, large flocks of sheep, studs of splendid horses and people at work everywhere. On the poorer land on the hills numerous peasantry would be going about their arduous duties with a phlegmatic resignation common to peasants everywhere and in every age. At fairly regular intervals, towns, ranging in size from a few thousand inhabitants to London which probably had about twenty thousand, provided marketing, sporting and social amenities. They were linked with each other by a network of superb roads, designed primarily for military use but thronging with civilian traffic. It is true that much of the landscape was still covered with primaeval forest, though broad zones slashed on either side of the great roads prevented the forest cover from being used by bandits and highwaymen. And large areas of the Fens and similar marshlands in Somerset and elsewhere had been drained and brought under cultivation.

In the hilly west, mining was carried on in Cornwall, the Mendips and Wales, slaves working the mines under unpleasant conditions. Otherwise the hills were left to their aboriginal inhabitants, who organized their lives much as ever they did before the Romans appeared. North of York the military presence was paramount. Here were no villas and comparatively little civilian life of the Roman pattern. The Wall, with its forts and castles and the roads leading to it, was the most conspicuous and most populous feature. There must have been agriculture, to feed the quite considerable population, but the picture we get is of a restless and discontented people resentful of the army in their midst and continually intriguing to get rid of it. Nevertheless, the whole of lowland Scotland can be regarded as within the Roman sphere.

The British ports were filled with traffic, both from the Roman world and from the unsubdued lands to the east and west (Ireland). Roman ships did not confine themselves to the short Channel crossing; there is evidence of considerable seaborne trade between Bordeaux and the ports of Yorkshire, for example. And the refusal of the Romano-British to regard the sea as a frontier was, in the end, their undoing. Even when barbarian invaders had poured across Gaul, severing the direct links with Rome, they still persisted in regarding Britain as a Roman province, with Rome itself as their homeland. Time and again, when a British usurper was raised to the rank of emperor by the local legions, his first thought was to embark with his troops to the Continent, in order to stake his claim to the Empire as a whole, leaving Britain itself defenceless.

If the Romano-British could have broken with their traditional mode of thought and regarded themselves as an independent nation, centuries of chaos and misery might have been avoided. But the era of nationalism was not yet. And so the Romano-British faded from the picture, to make way for a less sophisticated, more barbarous but more vigorous race.

The Mens, 360 acres of natural woodland in Sussex, probably regenerated from the ancient forest of Andredsweald, now called The Weald. It is cared for by the Sussex Trust for Nature Conservation.

The mountains of the North. *Above:* Slioch, Ross-shire, 3,260 feet high, rises abruptly from Loch Maree. *Below:* Beinn Eighe, Ross-shire, 3,309 feet, noted for its white quartzite peaks. It is now a nature reserve.

Iron-Age forts of the lowlands. *Above:* White Castle Fort, above Garvald, East Lothian, on the eastern edge of the Lammermuir Hills. *Below:* Maiden Castle, Dorset, once stormed by the Roman army.

The mysterious remains of pre-history. *Above:* Stonehenge, Wiltshire. *Below:* Trevethy Quoit, near Liskeard, Cornwall – an ancient burial place.

Ancient ridgeway tracks. *Above:* The South Downs Way, on Windover Hill, Sussex. *Below:* Midland ridge and furrow, near Market Harborough, Leicestershire.

Roman remains. *Above:* The geometric floor at Fishbourne Palace, near Chichester, laid when the palace was built, probably about AD75. *Below:* The Roman road on Blackstone Edge, above Rochdale, Lancashire.

Above: The west gate of Pevensey Castle, built by the Romans towards the end of the third century as one of the forts guarding 'the Saxon shore'. *Below:* Well-preserved Roman wall – Housesteads Fort lies beyond the first group of trees.

A Norse field pattern seen from Great Gable in the Lake District, looking west over Wasdale and Wastwater towards the Cumbrian coast.

4

From the Mists of the Dark Ages

After sharing the fortunes of the Roman world for nearly four hundred years, Britain shared its fate when the Empire collapsed. The decline and fall of the Roman Empire is perhaps best seen as a process of evolution rather than as a complete relapse into barbarism. For centuries before the Teutonic tribes poured over the frontier into the western world, they had been familiar neighbours. For much of the time there was peaceful trading across the Rhine and the Danube, which were the official frontiers of the Roman Empire. But quite often the tribes of the German forests and plains, frequently at war with each other, would unite for a brief period under some outstanding leader and would raid Roman provinces. The Romans would then mount an expedition across the boundary and penetrate deep into enemy territory, though with varying success, for as early as AD 9 the Germans under Hermann entirely annihilated three legions under the General Varus. The Roman army marched into the Teutoburger Forest and was never heard of again.

German soldiers were also familiar members of the Roman armies, which relied heavily on auxiliaries. For an adventurous and energetic young man, the service offered an interesting and potentially profitable career, and there was no racial barrier. The Roman system tolerantly absorbed all races and cultures, without distinction. One of the most important attractions was that an enlisted soldier, after serving for twenty-five years, was retired with a large gratuity, probably a substantial grant of land and, above all, Roman citizenship. The soldiers who helped to conquer Britain and later settled in the *coloniae* doubtless included some from virtually every province of the Empire, from Egypt and Mesopotamia to Spain and Mauretania. With Britain incorporated into the Empire, soldiers of British birth helped to fight the Roman wars in distant countries; we know, for instance, that several battalions of Britons were serving under the Emperor Trajan when he added Dacia (Rumania) to the Empire in AD 106. During the Roman era, therefore, the population of Britain came near to being cosmopolitan, and it is not surprising to find archaeological evidence of Saxon settlements, as in the neighbourhood of Dorchester-on-Thames, at quite early dates.

The chief military threat to Roman Britain was regarded as coming from the North and West rather than the East, though the North Sea was infested with Saxon pirates. The northern tribes broken through the Wall in 155–158 and again, with apparently much greater devastation, in AD 196: Between the years 287 and 296 two usurpers, Carausius and Allectus, ruled Britain as an independent state. Carausius was an admiral and, as his authority was based on sea power, he included in his 'empire' the coasts of the Netherlands. He also established along the southern and eastern shores of Britain, from Norfolk to the Isle of Wight, a line of fortresses under the command of an officer known as 'The Count of the Saxon Shore'. The implication of the title is that the Saxon pirates were beginning to be troublesome. In the year 367 the tribes of the north and west, the Picts and the Scots of history books, made common cause with the Saxons. They broke through the Wall, defeated the Roman army and killed the Count of the Saxon Shore. For about a year raiders moved about Britain almost unchecked, pillaging and killing and being joined by escaped slaves with accounts of their own to settle. The province never completely recovered from this disaster, though energetic measures by a Roman general, Theodosius, restored the military situation.

Meantime, the main body of the Empire was experiencing similar troubles. The Teutonic tribes were under increasing pressure from the rear, as nomadic nations moved westwards from the steppes of central Asia, where apparently the grasslands were drying up. Similar irruptions had occurred in earlier periods, but the coming of the Huns was the most catastrophic of all and caused terror throughout Europe. The Huns were a savage tribe of horsemen of Mongolian origin, ugly and unprepossessing by European standards but possessing undoubted military ability. In frantic endeavours to escape, Teutonic tribes, such as the Goths, presented themselves at the frontiers and asked to be allowed to move in and settle under Roman protection. When permission was refused, they moved in just the same. In the year 378 the Goths crossed the Danube and defeated a Roman army at Adrianople. In 406 the Vandals marched across the frozen Rhine in the depth of winter and poured through Gaul, then into Spain and North Africa. In 410 Rome itself was sacked by Alaric, the Goth. Within a few decades the old order had been replaced by a new one, in which Teutonic kings reigned over independent kingdoms in territories which had until recently been Roman provinces. When in 451 Attila, the Hun, invaded the West, he was finally checked at 'The Battle of the Nations' near Chalons-sur-Marne by a huge combined force of Roman and Teutonic armies.

Over much of the Roman world the transition was so sudden that it made little difference to the population. Many towns were sacked, but others escaped. Peasants in the fields, if they could keep out of the way of armies on passage, carried on with their accustomed tasks. The newcomers, though warlike and militarily efficient, were not numerous. What they did was to impose a new aristocracy on the countries they occupied. For ordinary people, it was simply an exchange of masters. In some instances it worked out as a change for the better, from the common citizen's point of view. The Vandals in Africa, after an initial period of wanton destruction, settled down to a life of indolence, in which their Teutonic energy soon atrophied. Under their lax rule, life went on much as before.

This did not happen in Britain. In the almost complete absence of contemporary records, it is difficult to establish why the pattern should have been so different, but certain surviving clues and much patient research enable us to suggest an answer.

It seems that the success of the barbarian invasions of the Continent inspired the Anglo-Saxons to mount a similar one of Britain. The popular version of the story is that, after the last Roman armies had evaporated, Britain was ruled for a time by a Celtic king named Vortigern. Harassed by the Scots and Irish, he adopted the familiar Roman device of bribing

others of his enemies to fight them. He introduced a
contingent of Saxons (or Jutes), who chased away the
northern raiders and were then given the Isle of Thanet as a
reward. Having spied out the weakness and also the
desirability of the country, the Jutes proceeded, after due
preparation, to take it over. Their leader was a man named
Hengist.

The date assigned to the arrival of Hengist is 449. As we
have seen, 451 marked the defeat or check of the Huns at
Chalons, in a battle in which Saxon contingents are known to
have been in the combined Roman and Teutonic armies. It is
at least possible that there is a connection between the two
events. Hengist may even have been sent by the Roman
general, Aëtius, to hold Britain while the campaign was in
progress.

He began his career as conqueror in 455 but was still
apparently fighting in Kent nearly twenty years later. Another
Saxon invasion by sea occurred in Sussex in 477 but Pevensey
(Anderida) was not captured till 491. Yet another wave of
immigrants landed in Southampton Water in 495, led by an
enigmatic character, Cerdic, who has a Celtic name and is the
reputed ancestor of every English monarch since, but he too
made little headway for many years.

Archaeological evidence indicates Saxon settlement in the
upper Thames valley at an early date, and the Wansdyke, an
impressive earthwork and ditch which extends across central
Wiltshire, from Bath eastwards, and which faces north, seems
to belong to the late fifth or early sixth century. Then the
Saxon tide seems to have been turned.

This is the era of the half-legendary Arthur. According to
modern historians, he represents the last resurgence of the old
Roman military prowess. He was not a king but a *dux bellorum*
(battle leader), a general of the old Roman school. His Roman
name would have been Artorius. His twelve battles against the
Saxons are well known, and much ingenuity has been
expended in trying to identify the sites. They seem to have
been well distributed throughout the country, and a recent
theory is that Arthur owed much of his success to an
importation of heavy cavalry horses. It was their heavy cavalry
which enabled the Goths to win the battle of Adrianople (see
above), and the lesson was not lost on the Romans. The

Saxons, though expert seamen, had little experience of horses and were quickly demoralized by attacks from well-trained contingents of armoured horsemen, moving swiftly along the Roman roads. There is some evidence that the Saxons actually withdrew right across Britain. In Cambridgeshire the Devil's Dyke and the Fleam Dyke probably belong to this period, thrown up by retreating Saxons against pursuing British armies. Some of the invaders seem to have returned to the Continent, where, in the ninth century, there was a tradition that Saxons living in a part of Thuringia were descended from migrants who had been driven out of Britain. When, more than fifty years later, the Saxons again came to the Wansdyke, probably advancing from the south instead of the north, they knew nothing of its history and so attributed it to their god, Woden.

So, the initial attempt of the Teutons, represented by the Anglo-Saxons, to possess Britain by one massive, co-ordinated campaign was foiled by the last great Romano-British general Artorius. After the climactic battle of Mount Badon, in or about the year 503, a period of peace endured for about forty years. It was ended, says tradition, by an internecine war among the Britons, which resulted in the death of Arthur in battle. Thereafter the Saxon advance was soon resumed.

But the original impetus had been lost. Instead of being accomplished in a few decades, the conquest of Britain now occupied more than 250 years. It was a piecemeal affair, in which Saxon kings fought each other as often as the British kings of the fragmented Celtic kingdoms, and in which, especially in the later years, British and Saxon kings quite frequently made common cause against a neighbour.

This had a highly significant effect on the development of the Britain that was to become England. On the Continent the transition had been so sudden that there was little break with tradition. In our own country it was so prolonged and so thorough that comparatively little survived of the old order. Towns were abandoned, villas crumbled into ruin, the very names of places were lost for ever. And the new civilization that was to replace the old was hammered together, slowly and painfully, from innumerable small, independent units. Eventual unity was built up from below instead of being imposed from above.

The countryside, therefore, was very extensively reshaped during the long centuries of the Anglo-Saxon conquest. Generalizations are treacherous, but it must be true to say that over much of the country the invaders eventually moved into virtually empty territory. If the population of Roman Britain at its zenith amounted to something over a million, it must have dwindled very considerably in succeeding centuries. Wars and pestilence took a heavy toll (an epidemic known as 'The Yellow Plague' ravaged Britain in 548 and resulted in a mortality which seems to have put it into the same category as the mediaeval Black Death). So many shiploads of Roman Britons, despairing of any future for the province, migrated to Armorica that that part of Gaul was subsequently called 'Brittany'. Over much of the country, though not everywhere, there is no continuity at all between the former Roman civilization and the Anglo-Saxon settlement.

The pattern of events is well illustrated in the chalk country of southern and eastern England. Here was a countryside populous and intensively cultivated in the pre-Roman era, though with cultivation restricted largely to the open downs. As we have seen, the Romans built their villas and carved out agricultural estates on the lower, more fertile land in the same districts, they and the peasants of the hills flourishing for a long time side by side, with little contact with each other. The catastrophe of the Saxon invasion apparently struck both equally. Both the villas and the villages were abandoned. Few coins of later than the fourth century AD have been found on any excavated sites. Only very few modern villages in the chalk country, such as Ashmore in Dorset and Winterslow in Wiltshire, have hill-top sites, indicating perhaps some continuity with Roman Britain, and villa sites were quickly submerged by the returning forest.

The Anglo-Saxons came up the rivers in their small boats and formed their early settlements on the river banks. Possibly the boats were retained as a means of retreat, should the settlement be threatened. What resulted was a kind of ribbon development, with the river instead of a road as a highway. As time went on, the river valleys became occupied by an almost continuous string of villages, from mouth to source. Packed in as tightly as possible, their only scope for expansion was uphill. The farms extended their territory inland from the river. In due course, each farm came to consist of a meadow or two by the river, a zone of cultivated fields on the gentle slopes above the meadows, and an area of downland on the sides and top of the hill. It would thus constitute a narrow strip of territory, no more than one or two fields broad but sometimes four to six miles long. Such is the shape of innumerable downland farms even today. When the villages became organized into parishes, at the coming of Christianity, the parishes assumed the same shape, which is still characteristic of most chalkland parishes. The farm or parish would keep extending its limits in the only direction it could go until it met the farmers of the next valley engaged in a similar expansion. So the entire countryside became parcelled out. And careful examination shows that the boundaries thus established took little or no account of former Romano-British villages on the hills, indicating that these had probably been deserted long ago.

Like the Belgae, the Anglo-Saxons came equipped with a heavy plough, capable of dealing with stiff soils. The valley lands presented them with no insuperable difficulties. Such a plough, however, is heavy and cumbersome, being in particular difficult to turn round. The tendency was, therefore, to plough in long strips, rather than in the small rectangular blocks of the former downland villages. The old English measurement of the furlong is derived from 'furrow-long'. The plough also required a team of oxen, as many as six or eight on heavy soils, and that was more oxen than any one owner, unless a particularly wealthy man, was likely to possess. The Anglo-Saxon settlements were therefore founded on mutual help. The inhabitants of any one settlement were of one people. Generally they were a family, descended from a common ancestor. The characteristic is preserved in many place-names incorporating the suffix 'ing'. Rustington is the 'town' of the Rusting family; Wokingham, the 'home' of the Wokings; Billingford, the ford of the Billings. Thus the names of the early settlers are perpetuated in numerous English villages.

Most English villages (many of which afterwards grew into towns) were so founded in the sixth, seventh and eighth centuries. Early documents, such as the grants of land given by Saxon kings to abbeys, carry lists of identifiable names. When we read the story of Alfred the Great's campaigns against the Danes, it can come as a shock to see small Somerset villages mentioned quite casually as they feature in the story. Here Aller, a tiny place on the edge of the marshes, is chosen as the venue for the baptism of Guthrum, the Danish king, after the battle of Ethandune. The year is 878. The village has a church and has probably been in existence for at least one hundred and perhaps two hundred years. There is no further documentary mention of Aller for another three hundred years, but undoubtedly it continued to house generations of farming folk, as it still does.

Despite the squalor in which they lived in their muddy lands along the Friesian and North German coasts, the Anglo-Saxons came to Britain with strong and pronounced ideas of personal freedom. It is true that there were slaves in their economy, but these belonged to subject peoples – in Britain the survivors of the Romano-British or Celts. Among themselves they held to the principles of equality, as befitted members of a family or clan. Their system of cultivating land therefore was based on communal effort, though, as already noted, that was partly due to the necessity of pooling resources of oxen. Wherever possible, they divided the land of the settlement into several large fields, on which they practised a three-course rotation. In the first year wheat was grown, in the second year barley, and in the third year the land lay fallow but was often grazed by cattle and sheep in summer. Each of the great fields was divided into a series of long, narrow strips, often only a few yards wide – again to fit the accepted ploughing pattern. The strips were allotted to the various families, in accordance with their needs, status and labour supplied. But, in general, no person could have two adjoining strips. They were allocated to give every household a proportion of the better land and a proportion of the poorer. In some instances, there seems to have been a new allocation every year. Thus, while the individual farmer had no choice as to the crop he would grow (except in the garden plot around his hut), much would depend on his own timely efforts throughout the year.

This system endured throughout much of the Middle Ages and in some districts even longer. The baulks into which the fields were divided are clearly visible in many a parish, especially in the Midlands. And at Laxton and the Isle of Axholme, on the borders of Nottinghamshire and Lincolnshire, the open fields survive to this day.

A visit to Laxton will demonstrate that the English countryside looked very different in Anglo-Saxon times from what it does today. It must have been a bare, open patchwork of fields, much like the hedgeless open fields of continental Europe. The only hedges or fences are likely to have been those around the wooden huts or houses.

Beyond the zone of arable fields lay the waste. In the downland regions already mentioned this would have been hill turf. Elsewhere it is most likely to have been forest. Over much of Britain an early English settlement would have resembled an island in an immense ocean of trees. Here cattle foraged under the supervision of the village cow-herd; or sheep grazed under the watchful eye of the shepherd; or the swineherd took the pigs rooting for grubs, roots, fallen berries and acorns. The waste was 'common' land, claimed by the community but not by any individual. In later times the rights of the various members of the community on the commons became defined and regulated. A household would have the right to pasture so many cattle, sheep, pigs or geese on the common. But the right was always associated with a holding, farm or property, never with a person. Such common rights still exist and are, in many instances, jealously guarded in many parts of the country.

In some regions, particularly eastern and south-eastern England, part of the common lay in the centre of the village and formed the village green, around which the houses were built. The Anglo-Saxons were a gregarious race, or perhaps the need for security made them so, and most of their early villages are fairly well nucleated, though, as noted, in downland areas the nucleus was elongated alongside a stream. As the settlers penetrated into forest and waterlogged country, they tended to choose hill rather than valley sites, a feature which prevails in much of Midland England. Later, when they began to occupy the formerly Celtic West and North, the initiative seems to have come more often from individual farmers, though perhaps under instructions from a superior. Devon in particular has a large number of isolated farms and hamlets dating from fairly late Saxon times. It looks as though when the Saxons invaded Devon in strength in the seventh century, they first settled in a limited number of large nucleated villages and then, as the countryside became more peaceful and the danger of British reprisals faded, established satellite farms and hamlets in vacant territory. The point that much of Devon is pasture land and unsuitable for ploughing is also relevant. A farmer specializing in livestock was not dependent on his neighbours for co-operation in such communal efforts as ploughing with a full team of oxen.

It is therefore fair to claim that in many parts of the country not only villages but also individual farms, and in some instances even the pattern of fields that compose the farms, date from Saxon times.

In later Saxon and mediaeval centuries, the standard unit of land is the 'hide'. From the point of view of scholarly research, this is a confusing measurement, for it apparently means the amount of land reckoned to be necessary for the support of a household. It therefore varies from district to district, ranging from about forty acres to over 120. However, once the custom for the district has been established, it is possible to compare pretty closely the size and extent of individual farms or manors with their modern counterparts. How well the two agree is often surprising.

In the troubled centuries following the first attempts at conquest, the Anglo-Saxon settlements tended to lose much of their original independence. With dangers threatening all around, the only hope of safety lay in co-operation with powerful neighbours, or with offering such neighbours certain concessions in return for protection. About the only form of tribute that a protector could be sure of getting was labour. So, as the little English kingdoms developed and expanded, the idea of service to an overlord took root. The farmer held his land in return for certain duties. The evolution of the feudal system was beginning.

In early Saxon times the blood feud probably prevailed. As the country became more settled, this was replaced by a system of fines. Virtually every crime could be compounded for by a money payment. Early Saxon laws, for instance, lay down the precise payments to be made for killing a man, the schedule being scaled according to the man's status – a hundred shillings for an independent farmer, three hundred shillings for a nobleman, forty shillings for a serf. Ina, the Wessex king who annexed Devon, estimated the 'wergild', or blood money, for a free Welshman (Briton) at 120 shillings, which was rather more than half the price he put on a free Englishman. The significant point, though, is that the law was taking over from anarchy. That implied courts and meetings for the administration of justice. An early judicial unit was the 'hundred', about the nature of which some controversy has existed. The accepted opinion is that the term referred to a hundred families or perhaps a hundred fighting men. In view of the above definition of a 'hide', it could thus have a territorial implication, but topographically the hundred units tend to be awkward. They endured well into the nineteenth century, when they were used as the basis for the establishment of workhouses, and so their boundaries are well known. They fit into a map like the units of an extremely complex jigsaw puzzle, with many anomalies and outlying splinters. Nevertheless, they remain an interesting link with the Anglo-Saxon world. It is presumed that the men of each hundred met for deliberations at regular intervals, and the identity of some of the meeting-places is known. Not far from my present home in Somerset is a spot known as The Hundred Stone, which was one such locality. It is, interestingly, not far from a minor Roman road.

Christianity survived the Roman Empire in Britain. Before the end of the Roman era there were British dioceses and bishops. From the age of Arthur a triad has survived which lists three Perpetual Choirs, where singers in relays sang praises around the clock, like modern factory workers on a shift system. The choirs are, incidentally, those of Llan Iltud Vawr (in Glamorgan), Amesbury and Glastonbury. Of them, the first and last were not incorporated into English kingdoms until the Anglo-Saxons had accepted Christianity. At Glastonbury it is known that the take-over was peaceable, the British abbot being left in office till the end of his days.

In general, however, there was friction between the British Church and the Catholicism introduced to south-eastern England by Augustine (who arrived in Kent in 597). The Catholic Church eventually prevailed, getting the better of the argument in the Synod of Whitby (663), but the British

Christians returned to their western homes defeated but not entirely convinced. As the new religion took hold among the Anglo-Saxons, an ecclesiastical administration parallel to the secular one was set up. British Christianity had veered towards monasticism. Its great men were abbots, not bishops. But among the Anglo-Saxons a system of dioceses and parishes was evolved.

So to Anglo-Saxon times belong not only the sites of the villages and their individual farms but the sites of their churches. In only a few instances have Anglo-Saxon churches survived, and those belong to the later period, when building in stone became common, but most rural parish churches are on sites selected by the first missionaries. And very often those were sites sacred to the displaced pagan religion.

The eighth century was, on the whole, a time of happy and peaceful development in England. Wars between the various kingdoms, both English and Celtic, flared up from time to time, but between were long periods of tranquillity. With the people now Christianized, the arts of civilization began to blossom. Men were composing poetry, writing books, creating music, painting pictures, erecting more ambitious buildings. Trade flourished, and the English kingdoms were in close diplomatic contact with the continent of Europe, where the great Charlemagne had organized a new empire, the Holy Roman Empire. It was an early renaissance, a false dawn.

Towards the end of the century a new set of pirates from across the North Sea began to torment the coastal towns of Britain. In the next century, the squalls grew to tornado strength, engulfing the whole of western Europe in new abyss of barbarism. It was the era of the Northmen, known more commonly in England as the Danes.

Before their onslaught civilization virtually collapsed. Almost everything achieved and won over the preceding centuries was lost. The story of how Alfred, the heroic king of Wessex, at last retrieved victory from almost complete disaster is well known. His renown, however, is due not only to his military victories but to his patient rebuilding of civilization from the wreck, a task in which he was engaged during the last twenty years of the ninth century.

In those years, while he was restoring the Church, writing books, codifying laws, encouraging trade and learning and doing all that one man could to lay the foundations of a new civilization, he was ably supported by his son and heir, Edward the Elder, who continued to conduct military campaigns against the still restless and formidable Northmen. In the process Edward carried on a policy initiated by Alfred and in so doing made a large contribution to the shaping of England.

Alfred had rightly gauged that the strength of the Northmen lay in their mobility. When cornered and forced to fight, they could be beaten by Englishmen. Their favourite tactics were the lightning raid, either from the sea or on requisitioned horses. They struck suddenly, killed, burned and departed with their loot before the English forces could gather. Alfred therefore built a series of strong points, fortified by earthworks and timber, in which the people could take refuge at the first sign of danger and which would serve as rallying-points for the part-time militia (the 'fyrd'). He called them 'burhs' or 'boroughs' and established about twenty-five of them in the part of England that remained to him.

His son Edward extended this policy. In the peace which Alfred made with the Danish King Guthrum, the boundary between Alfred's kingdom and the Danelaw, as the Danish-controlled region was called, was fixed as "the mouth of the Thames westwards to the junction with the River Lea; then up the Lea to its source; then in a straight line to Bedford; and from thence along the River Ouse to Watling Street, which from that point served as the frontier to the mouth of the River Dee". It served as a theoretical boundary, though whenever the Danes thought they saw an opportunity, they raided across it. So Edward carried the war to the enemy. Throughout Midland England up to Watling Street, he established boroughs of the same type as those of Old Wessex, and then he penetrated beyond the frontier and employed the same strategy there. He was ably seconded by his brother-in-law, Ethelred, whom Alfred had made Earl of Mercia, and, after Ethelred's death, by his widow, Ethelfleda, one of the outstanding women in English history, who well deserved her affectionate title, 'The Lady of Mercia'. *The Anglo-Saxon Chronicle* gives a list of some of the fortresses she built: Tamworth, Stafford, Eddisbury, Warwick, Chirbury, Warburton, Runcorn. Bridgnorth was another of her foundations, and she refortified the old Roman town of Chester. Among the places built, fortified, founded or rebuilt by Edward are Huntingdon, Manchester, Bakewell, Towcester, Maldon (in Essex) and Hertford. Most of the boroughs thus established by Alfred, Edward and Ethelfleda became in due course towns, and in the reign of King Edgar (957–75) many of them became the headquarters of the shires into which the country was then divided, superseding the old Anglo-Saxon kingdoms. The pattern by which England was administered for over a thousand years was thus initiated by Alfred and his immediate successors.

The Danes, Northmen or Vikings were by instinct traders. They much preferred to take the commodities in which they traded by force rather than buy them, but when that was not possible, they engaged in more legitimate transactions. They had a well-established trade route, via the rivers of Russia, to the Arab kingdoms of the Middle East. Trade is best carried on in towns, and so wherever they settled they established towns. The earliest towns in Ireland were of Danish foundation. In England the five principal towns of the Danelaw were Derby, Nottingham, Leicester, Lincoln and Stamford. York also became a major Viking stronghold. Later, when the Northmen brought over their families to settle as agriculturists, they founded in north-eastern England hundreds of villages whose origin is still demonstrated by the suffixes 'by', 'thorpe', 'wick', 'toft' and other northern elements. The administrative divisions had different names, some of which are still used. In north-eastern England we find 'wapentakes' instead of 'hundreds'; the district around Peterborough is still known as the Soke of Peterborough; and the three major divisions of Yorkshire were until recently the 'Ridings', derived from 'thirdings'.

The contribution of the Dark Ages to the shaping of the countryside is thus the provision of a framework for the future. The age was too destructive to produce many great buildings, but it determined the sites of very many future ones.

The Anglo-Saxons, however, carved their signature on the landscape in the form of several great earthworks which still survive. The Wansdyke has already been mentioned, as have the Devil's Dyke and Fleam Dyke in Cambridgeshire. Another major work is Offa's Dyke, constructed by the Mercian King Offa in the eighth century as a frontier between Mercia and Wales. It is an impressive undertaking, extending from the North Wales coast near Prestatyn to the mouth of the Severn near Chepstow. Offa's Mercia must have been both populous and prosperous to be able to excavate it.

Earlier in the period some of the old hill-top fortresses, abandoned at the beginning of the Roman era, were refortified. One such is Cadbury Castle, in south-eastern Somerset, which is traditionally identified as the 'Camelot' of the Romano-British hero, Arthur. Excavations in recent years have indicated that it was indeed re-occupied and refortified during the Dark Ages and may well have been the headquarters of a notable chieftain such as Arthur.

The Saxons also used old hill-forts as places of assembly, examples being Badbury Rings and Eggardon, in Dorset. Such meeting-places they called 'moots'. Any natural feature, such as a large tree or a standing stone, could be utilized for a rendezvous, and there are some instances of old tumuli being so employed. In pre-Christian days, however, the Saxons themselves constructed barrows over their dead, one particularly notable example being at Sutton Hoo, Suffolk, from which a splendid treasure of a seventh-century king has been recovered.

Other relics of the obscure centuries that followed the Roman withdrawal are the numerous stone crosses which may still be seen in villages, churchyards and fields, chiefly in Celtic districts. There are many in Cornwall and in Scotland and northern England. Many are profusely decorated with carving, which becomes especially ornate in crosses of the Danish period in the North, where Celtic and Danish motifs are intricately mingled. In general, Celtic crosses have a circle around the cross, whereas Saxon examples do not. In the North some crosses bear runic or ogham inscriptions. Before Augustine reintroduced the link with Rome, Christianity came to northern Britain via Ireland in the persons of missionaries of the stamp of St Columba. While much of the masonry of Iona Abbey, where Columba made his headquarters for the conversion of Scotland, is of a later date, the remains of his stone cell can still be seen. Similar cells occur in many other districts in which Celtic missionaries worked; there are, for instance, over two hundred sites known on the Isle of Man.

It is as well to remember that throughout most of the period the lowlands of Scotland shared the same history as northern England. Neither Hadrian's Wall nor the Tweed constituted a frontier. For centuries south-eastern Scotland was an integral part of the Anglian kingdom of Northumbria, Edinburgh itself being the 'borough of Edwin', a Northumbrian king. The western side and the islands remained Celtic, much of it being included in the Celtic kingdom of Strathclyde until old political divisions were obliterated by the coming of the Northmen. It is interesting to reflect that one of the northernmost counties of Scotland, Sutherland, was regarded as the 'southern land' by the new invaders. Until their arrival, the Highlands had retained independence. A feature of the Pictish Highlands is the 'broch', a round fortress-tower of which a number of examples survive. One excavated in recent years at Clickhimin, in the Shetland Isles, revealed itself as a communal dwelling, two or three storeys high, facing inwards to an open courtyard. Although this particular broch dates back to the second or third century BC, similar buildings, serving apparently as primitive tenements, were in use until much more recent times.

5

The Normans and the Middle Centuries

To the Anglo-Saxons of 1066 the Norman invasion must have
seemed a continuation of the wars against the Vikings, which
had been dragging on for the past two hundred years. Under
Alfred the Great and his successors the English had been
victorious; under Ethelred II they had been ignominiously
defeated. They had lived under a Danish king, Canute, then
under an English king again, Edward the Confessor. Now the
Northmen were back again. It was wearisome repetition of an
old familiar theme.

In that fateful year which so many history books take,
erroneously, as the beginning of English history, there were
indeed two invasions. First the Northmen, under Harald
Hardrada, King of Norway, landed in the North and were
defeated and killed by the English king, Harold. Then, within
a few days, William of Normandy landed in Pevensey Bay,
and he, too, might well have been likewise beaten, if only the
impetuous Harold had waited till he had gathered his full
forces before attempting battle. The Northmen and the
Normans – basically, the same people.

The fundamental difference was that the Normans had
been living in France for more than a hundred years. They
were descendants of Viking pirates and adventurers who, after
thoroughly devastating Normandy and the neighbouring
provinces, had settled there. These restless, vigorous,
intelligent rovers were nothing if not adaptable. Within a very
few generations they had absorbed much of the old culture of
the land in which they had settled. By the time William
launched on his adventure across the Channel, they were
almost more French than the French. With the Norman
Conquest, therefore, England was decisively and irretrievably

brought back within the European comity of nations. For the next few centuries both shores of the English Channel were, as often as not, ruled by the same king. The fortunes of our islands were firmly linked with those of the European continent rather than with those of the sea-kings of the North.

The numbers engaged in battle at Hastings were not great. Probably the English outnumbered the Normans, but the latter were mostly armed knights, who fought on horseback, whereas the English dismounted and formed a shield wall. Five to six thousand Normans, plus a thousand or two archers, against eight to ten thousand English is a modern estimate, though some authorities think there were fewer on both sides. The Norman army was a heterogeneous crowd, brought together by the promise of booty. Many were from Normandy, many, too, from Brittany and southern regions of France, some from Spain and Norman Italy. They were adventurers all, proposing to collect their share of the spoil or to die in the attempt.

When, therefore, the battle was won and the share-out began, these were the men among whom England was divided. Manor by manor, village by village, the country was parcelled out. Alien knights, speaking no English, duly arrived to take possession of their new property, a process which often involved ousting the bereaved family of an English aristocrat who had fallen at Hastings. Understandably, there was bitter resentment. The new landlord could only hope to survive by emulating the strictness of his master, William. And by surrounding himself with strong walls and a loyal bodyguard.

So began the age of castles. The first ones were hurriedly constructed of earth and timber. Their sites appear now as mottes, which are flat-topped cones of earth surrounded by a deep ditch. The platform thus created was defended by a timber palisade. In the middle was a square tower which served as an ultimate defence but, when not under siege, acted as a residence, stable, storehouse and watch-tower. The whole was a military post, designed to hold a hostile land in order, and was occupied by the knight and his personal band of retainers, which might well include a small contingent of those archers who had been so effective at Hastings. No doubt for a time the law of the sword was supreme.

But however arrogant these new masters of England might

be, they themselves had a master. William was a stern, violent and terrible man who would tolerate no challenge to his authority. In the year of his death *The Anglo-Saxon Chronicle* comments, in awe, "He had earls in his fetters ... he expelled bishops from their sees, and abbots from their abbacies ... and finally he did not spare his own brother, Odo, ... but put him in prison." The chronicler adds, "Any honest man could travel over his kingdom without injury with his bosom full of gold; and no one dared strike another, however much wrong he had done him."

The peace thus imposed by fear gave the country a breathing-space to recover from the traumatic events of 1066. That the English appreciated the severe but reasonably just rule of the Conqueror is illustrated by the fact that when a rebellion occurred in the Midlands in 1075, the English militia supported the King, in spite of the fact that one of the leaders of the revolt was an Englishman, Waltheof. Because they felt themselves oppressed by their new local lords, it was good to know that there was someone who could keep even these petty tyrants in order.

The comparative peace also gave the new local gentry time to consolidate their position. There was leisure to strengthen the defences of the new castles and to replace timber with stone. In the years that followed, this process continued until castles became like small towns and then in their turn were rendered obsolete by the age of explosives. The most notable example of Norman castles of William I's reign is, of course, the Tower of London, erected, like every other castle, to keep the local population in proper subservience. Mottes and ditches are now usually all that remain of the earlier Norman castles, and they are particularly numerous in the counties along the Welsh border.

The Normans were great administrators, and none more efficient than William. He was king by right of conquest, and what he had, he intended to hold. Every one of the manors now possessed by his followers was his personal gift to them. Nor was it an outright gift. They held it in return for service to him. In short, the whole land belonged to the king. The feudal system was thus firmly established in England. Every man had his place in the system and held that place by virtue of service to his superiors.

With the instincts of a bureaucrat, William had it all set down in writing. In 1086 he caused an inventory, the Domesday Book, to be made of all his vast possessions, meaning not only land under his direct control but land occupied by his subjects. Writes the Anglo-Saxon chronicler, awestricken but disapproving, "So narrowly did he cause the survey to be made that there was not one single hide nor rood of land, nor – it is shameful to tell but he thought it no shame to do – was there an ox, cow or swine that was not set down in the writ." Knowledge is power, and the detailed knowledge of his realm which William thus acquired was unmatched in his time anywhere, and for a long time afterwards.

From our point of view, the Domesday Book is invaluable, giving as it does an almost complete picture of England in his reign. As a matter of fact, it supplies a picture of the realm not only in 1086 but in 1066, for the cryptic letters which continually crop up, " T.R.E. ", refer to the time of Edward the Confessor, to "the day when King Edward was alive and dead", as the contemporary phrase has it. Virtually every entry in the Book can be matched with a known locality on the modern map; and most English parish histories begin with Domesday. We can identify the manors, map in some instances their very boundaries and make shrewd guesses as to where the farmers ('villeins' as they were called) lived. And one interesting fact that emerges is that the changes caused by the Norman Conquest were chiefly at the higher levels of society. At the rural or peasant level there is little difference between the England of 1066 and 1086.

A celebrated or notorious aspect of William's character was his love of hunting. "He preserved the harts and boars and loved the tall stags as if he were their father. He also appointed concerning the hares that they should go free. The rich complained and the poor murmured, but he was so sturdy that he recked nought of them." Great areas of England were designated royal forests or chases, and the severe forest laws applied to them included blinding as a punishment for poaching. That whole districts were cleared of their agricultural population in order to make a forest is unlikely, but it is true that by the twelfth century nearly one-third of the total acreage of England was royal forest.

When viewed from the contemporary angle rather than our

own, however, the situation seems more reasonable. In the first place, the country was governed on the principle that it belonged to the king. Much of it he let out to tenants in return for specified services, but the royal chases he kept for his own use. Secondly, when we consider what those uses were, we shall find that the royal household was cropping the wild animals of the forest in much the same way as hunters now crop the big game of Africa. The mediaeval Court was peripatetic. The king with his retinue moved around the country not only to keep an eye on his subjects but also to eke out provisions. It was easier to move about to where supplies of food were available than to transport the food to a permanent capital. This was ancient practice, dating from the time of the early Saxon kings. The king would have manors or estates of his own dotted over the country, would descend on each in turn and would stay there for a few days or weeks until provisions became scarce. Then the cavalcade would move on, probably leaving the permanent residents on short commons for a time. At a much later date (the fifteenth century), Henry VII employed the principle of forced hospitality to ruin some of his potentially troublesome subjects, descending on them with his entire Court and staying until they were virtually bankrupt.

In these perambulations the chase played an important part. Without slaughtering an inordinate proportion of the local draught oxen, which would be extremely tough anyway, the chief source of meat would be wild animals from the forest – the deer, the wild boar and even the hares and rabbits (the last largely introduced by the Normans). Hunting deer and boar was a business-like undertaking. It was not a matter of galloping after them over miles of country. The sportsmen, armed with bows, stood in strategic positions at the edge of cover, and beaters drove the game towards them. (It was much like modern shooting of grouse or pheasants.) The animals of the chase were therefore not only regarded as the king's private property, ranging over his own land, but were also his dinner. Woe betide any foolhardy subject who had the temerity to steal the king's meat! Doubtless the Saxon peasant, accustomed to helping himself to the forest animals, saw things differently, but one can appreciate the king's point of view. And in many instances it is unlikely that the peasant had had free access to this wild game for a long time, for the Norman kings merely extended a practice that had been widely followed by the Saxon kings.

From the point of view of our theme, the shaping of the countryside, the establishment of the royal chases and their strict protection have preserved for us big areas of ancient forest which might otherwise have been lost to the plough. Vestiges of many of the sixty-nine royal chases in England still remain, one of the most extensive being, of course, the New Forest. Here a hundred thousand acres of woodland and heathland are much as they were in Norman times, and even earlier. It has been calculated that even the boundaries between forest and heath remain virtually unaltered. Two-thirds or thereabouts are open to the public, and over these extensive tracts the Forest commoners still exercise their ancient rights of pasturage, pannage, estover, turbary and the rest.

The following list of royal chases in the early Middle Ages gives some idea of how much we owe to them for the preservation of the forests of England.

In Southern England, a broad zone of forest land linked the New Forest with the Forest of Windsor, which itself occupied all of the southern bank of the Thames from Henley to Chertsey. Westwards the Forest of Windsor was connected by a continuous forest belt with Savernake and the Forest of Chute, and southwards another woodland zone extended, via Alice Holt and Wolmer Forest to Porchester. Along the Somerset/Wiltshire border stretched the great primaeval Forest of Selwood, linking up with the Forest of Blackmore in Blackmore Vale, with Bere Forest and Purbeck also royal chases in Dorset. In Somerset both Exmoor and Mendip were royal forests, while other considerable areas covered the hills near Taunton (Neroche) and North Petherton. Near Bristol was the Forest of Kingswood, and in north-west Wiltshire the Forest of Braden.

In the Midlands, a vast forest belt extended from the neighbourhood of Oxford (Wychwood and Shotover) north-eastwards by way of Bernwood, Whittlewood, Salcey and Rockingham to the Forest of Huntingdon, which covered the whole of the county of that name. Rutland was also largely occupied by the Forest of Rutland. Another forest zone extended in an arc around Stratford-on-Avon and Evesham Vale, the Forest of Arden being the best known sector. Others were Feckenham, Cannock Chase, Kinver, Wrekin, Morfe and, beyond the Severn, Shirlet and Long Forest. Nottingham, of course, had Sherwood. Also farther south the Forests of Dean and Irchenfield. The Peak of Derbyshire was forest country, adjoined on the west by the Forest of Macclesfield. In western Cheshire were the Forests of Delamere and the Wirral.

In the North, most of northern Lancashire was occupied by the Forest of Lonsdale and Amounderness. Across the Pennines the Forest of Galtres covered a big area north of York, while on the moors above the Vale of Pickering were the Forests of Pickering and Farndale. Two big forests, Allerdale and Inglewood, covered most of northern Cumberland. The Forest of Northumberland occupied much of the territory between the Wansbeck and the Cheviots.

In Scotland, the great Caledonian Forest still spread over much of the Highlands. Scotland was included in William I's realm; the time of the division of the kingdoms was not yet.

The forest laws were necessary because the pressure on land was already becoming strong. A careful estimate of the population of England and Wales at the time of the Domesday Book is 1,200,000, which may be much the same as it was at the zenith of the Roman era. That was approaching the comfortable limit for an economy based almost entirely on agriculture, especially if we exclude the royal chases and the other untamed forest areas (such as the Weald, which, although still densely wooded, was not a royal chase).

Apart from the advance of the plough, the forests were being diminished by the natural activities of grazing animals, especially cattle. Their hooves destroyed much of the woodland vegetation under the trees, encouraged the growth of grass and consolidated the soil, while they and sheep nibbled at the forest seedlings as they emerged and so prevented natural regeneration. Although, to judge from the instance of the New Forest, cattle were not entirely excluded from royal chases, at least their numbers were regulated.

As the population pressure increased, with more and more animals seeking their living from the waste, the enclosure of forest land developed. There are few records of actual early enclosures, but we know, for instance, that a section of the Forest of Northumberland (now 365 acres) was enclosed by a stone wall in about 1220 to form Chillingham Park. It trapped within its precincts a herd of wild white cattle which still flourish, the celebrated Chillingham Herd.

Apart from the terrible two decades of civil war, between Stephen and Matilda, and apart from occasional flare-ups between the armed nobility, the Middle Ages were, in England, a time of comparative peace. Hence, in spite of the low standard of living prevailing among the peasantry, the population almost trebled between 1086 and 1349, when, on the eve of the Black Death, it is held to have been between 3,500,000 and 4,000,000. A country with a population of that density needed the restrictions which the well-ordered feudal system imposed.

Our picture of mediaeval England is of a land of villages – the same villages that exist today. Each consists of a group of huts at a short but respectful distance from the castle (later the manor house) of the local lord. The huts are of split timber in well-forested districts and of wattle-and-daub with half-timbering in areas which have been denuded of forests. The huts have no windows or chimney, and the smoke from the open fire on the hearth escapes either through the doorway or through holes in the thatched roof. Each hut is surrounded by a small fenced enclosure, occupied by domestic animals and children and perhaps by vegetable plots.

A muddy track leads to the open fields, which are divided, as already noted, into three main sections and subdivided into narrow baulks or strips. In any one year one field will be bearing a crop of wheat, another oats or barley while the third lies fallow and is grazed by the village livestock. The villager has no choice in the matter of crops. No matter how many strips he holds in Field 1 (and the number depends on his wealth and status), he must grow wheat there, but his harvest can be influenced by the care and attention he gives to it. Cattle, sheep, pigs and geese are his personal property but graze on the village commons or browse through the forests under the care of a specialist herdsman or flockmaster. In addition to the three main fields, there is an area of meadowland, set aside for cutting for hay for winter use. All around this island of cultivation are primaeval forests or marshes, inhabited by deer and, in the early centuries, by such other alarming animals as wolves and wild cattle. Here the lord goes hunting. Hedges or hurdle fences are in some instances necessary to protect the cultivated fields from depredations by these forest denizens, but the barriers are erected around the fields as a whole, never between individual strips.

The lord is a farmer, like the peasants. He is allotted a share of the strips in the open fields, though a greater number than any of his neighbours because of his superior status. He does not, however, work on the land. The peasants are required to cultivate his strips for him. To each peasant holding are attached certain duties, notably the number of days' work that the peasant must put in on the lord's domain. To ensure that these duties are carried out, the lord employs a bailiff, who also has a house by the village street, larger perhaps than those of most of the peasants but of the same type. He too has strips in the arable fields and livestock on the common, and the peasants owe duties to him as well. The other noteworthy village resident is the priest, who lives in a hut like the peasants and has his strips of land in the fields, besides being entitled to a share of the produce from the peasants' plots. At the lowest end of the social scale are serfs, who are virtually slaves, working for their subsistence and without property, but this class gradually disappeared as the centuries passed. The system seems a harsh one, especially from the point of view of the peasant farmer, but it must be remembered that it was a virtually moneyless society. The dues which the peasant paid to his lord and his retainers can be compared to the taxes, direct and indirect, paid by his modern counterpart. If one translates them into the common denominator of time, it may well emerge that the modern artisan, tradesman or office-worker is left with less productive time for himself than his peasant ancestor had.

In general, there was no mobility of labour. The peasant was bound to his native village. He could not escape, but, on the other hand, neither could he be evicted. His world was bounded by the village fields and the encircling forest or waste. For enterprising young men, however, there were possibilities of enlarging their horizons. The lord of the manor had business outside the parish boundaries, and when he travelled he naturally took an impressive band of retainers with him. When the king's Court, on his perambulations around the kingdom, was in the vicinity, he would be required to attend. He would be called upon to bring contingents to aid the king in any foreign wars. There were also hundred courts and shire courts to be attended, and, after the realm had settled down under the Angevin kings, tournaments to be enjoyed.

Three features of mediaeval life played important roles in opening the eyes of the isolated villagers of the countryside to the outside world. They were the Crusades, the growth of fairs and markets, and pilgrimages.

The first crusade was launched in 1096, only thirty years after the Battle of Hastings, and others occupied, though with decreasing support and popularity, most of the Middle Ages. Formidable armies of knights with their retainers struggled across Europe to Byzantium (Constantinople) and thence into the heart of the mysterious East. For young men reared in the restricted environment of an English village, to embark on a crusade must have been an enlightening and traumatic experience. After such an expedition to the ends of the world, life would never be the same again.

Novelties and luxuries naturally began to flow back to western Europe. Surviving mediaeval account books for the port of Southampton, for instance, illustrate a thriving trade in such commodities as spices, sugar, dates, almonds, silks, damask, ivory, raisins and sweet wine. New ideas, too, began to circulate, ranging from philosophy and fashion to the architecture of castles. The later mediaeval castles, elaborately designed and almost impregnable, owe much to patterns borrowed by crusaders from the Eastern Empire.

The increase in trade naturally implied the growth of towns and cities, now feasible under the stronger central government which was more the rule than the exception. A money economy began to shape itself side by side with the feudal system, under which debts were paid in kind or in service. And the spirit of liberty, which is continually fermenting in the minds of men, impelled the towns to seek freedom and self-government. The crusades provided them with opportunities, especially in the reign of Richard I, who was constantly in need of money to finance his military ventures and, latterly, to ransom him from a German prison. Charters galore were granted in return for money payments. Some were charters of self-government, others were permissions to hold markets and fairs on certain days. At these events tolls were paid by everyone displaying produce for sale, and no business transactions could be legally made within a specified radius of the fair while it was being held. Some of the mediaeval fairs assumed impressive proportions. That of St Giles, at Winchester, for instance, originally lasted three days, according to a charter granted by William Rufus, but later charters by impecunious kings extended it to sixteen days, during which all trade within ten miles of the fair site, even in the city of Winchester, was suspended. The Fair itself took on the character of a vast town of booths, with temporary streets for each trade or industry.

The wealth engendered by such events was so obvious that it is no wonder that numerous landowners sought to cash in on them. It became the fashion for a lord of the manor to encourage the growth of a town on his land and to help the citizens to obtain rights for fairs, markets and other concessions. In his book *Devon and its People*, Professor W.G. Hoskins gives a number of examples of towns deliberately founded in this way. Some, such as Tavistock, Ashburton, Crediton, Honiton and Okehampton, flourished; others failed and still remain nothing but villages.

By the end of the Middle Ages, virtually every village in the country was within walking distance of a fair or market, and most villagers were able to make at least one annual visit to such an event. There they would not only be able to buy ribbons, haberdashery, cloth and other goods from stallholders but would be entertained by jugglers, cheapjacks, dancing bears and other travelling showmen. That many of the old fairs still survive is due largely to the descendants of these showmen, who determinedly insist on the maintenance of the old charters and customs, and many country folk still look forward to the fair as the traditional annual outing, even though they may visit the local town weekly on shopping expeditions.

Though their physical impact on the countryside has been therefore ephemeral, the fairs have played an important part in the development of rural life. As social occasions, their influence can hardly be exaggerated. And the associated growth of country towns has been responsible for the evolution of much of the network of country roads and lanes which so exasperates motorists in a hurry. If the Roman roads are masterpieces of imaginative strategic planning, the English lane represents an automatic response to local needs. Like so many other English institutions, no one ever planned it; it just grew.

Mediaeval people had another excuse for leaving their ancestral homes and taking to the roads. At some time in their lives many of them felt impelled to make a pilgrimage. Sometimes their journey into the unknown was undertaken as a penance imposed for a crime; sometimes it was in response to some mystical impulse; sometimes, we may guess, it arose from a desire for a holiday. The traditional destinations of pilgrims were Rome and Jerusalem, and it was due to infidel interference with Christian pilgrims to the latter shrine that the First Crusade was launched. Later the shrine of St James of Compostella, in north-western Spain attracted millions of pilgrims, who returned proudly wearing their cockleshell badge, the sign of an accomplished pilgrimage. After 1170 England had her own major goal for pilgrims, the shrine of St Thomas à Becket at Canterbury. Chaucer's *Canterbury Tales*, that early masterpiece of English literature, gives us a lively picture of the types of pilgrims who cantered over the grassy ridgeways of the North Downs on their way to Canterbury in the springtime.

So we come to the final agent in the shaping of the mediaeval countryside, the Church. We have already noted the village church as a central feature of each village, with the local priest playing his part in village affairs. That role varied immensely, according to the character of the priest. The average mediaeval peasant seems to have been pious, or probably superstitious would be a better word, but rough and ignorant, and it is not to be supposed that many priests were much different. King Alfred's dream of a literate nation was a long time in becoming a reality.

At the higher ecclesiastical levels, many bishops and archbishops faithfully mirrored their secular counterparts. The militant bishop, charging side by side with his knightly relations, is a familiar mediaeval figure. On the other hand, every generation has produced its saints. From the earlier days of Christianity in our islands we have the attractive picture of Aldhelm, missionary bishop to the West Saxons of Somerset, setting out at the age of seventy to explore his new diocese of Sherborne, his sturdy ash-stick in his hand and his harp slung over his shoulder. In the wild and bandit-ridden Forest of Selwood he would sit on a bridge, playing the harp and singing songs of his own composition until a crowd gathered. Then he would switch to psalms and preach a good, vigorous, hell-fire sermon. In a later century, the fourteenth, the friars launched on the world by the saintly Francis of Assisi championed the cause of the oppressed and poor and set Europe in a ferment. John Ball, whose preaching was one of the immediate causes of Wat Tyler's peasant revolt in 1381, was a parish priest.

That the Normans were great builders has already been demonstrated by their prolific construction of mighty castles. The same propensity found an outlet in the rebuilding of churches, on a scale matched only in Victorian times, if then. Most Saxon parish churches had been timber-built originally, and although during the reigns of the later Saxon kings some of them had been replaced by stone buildings, these were in a minority. The Normans and their successors made such a thorough job of erecting what they deemed more worthy edifices to the glory of God that very, very few Saxon churches remain.

The early Norman churches were, like the castles and the character of their builders, massive and solid. The walls were thick, the arches rounded, the towers squat. Succeeding centuries modified this style by discovering the potentialities of bisecting arches and so developed the splendid Gothic architecture of which we have so many fine examples in English churches and cathedrals. Later still the arches became more flattened, giving more window-space and so admitting more light. Stained-glass windows provided sermons for the illiterate, as did also vivid paintings of religious themes on mediaeval church walls. Morality plays performed on portable platforms at fairs and markets were part of the attractions of those occasions and were the embryo of the Elizabethan theatre.

Religion, to a greater extent than today, dominated the lives of ordinary villagers and citizens. In its early days Christianity, unable to wean an obstinately conservative people from their old pagan beliefs, had wisely adopted and adapted as many of the old traditions and customs as possible. Most of these were calendar customs, associated with the circle of the seasons and the rural activities dictated by them. So the festival of the spring equinox became Easter, after a Scandinavian goddess Eostre; the autumn equinox was dedicated to St Michael; the autumnal festival when ghosts and spirits wandered over the earth (Samhain) was transformed into All Saints' Day, allowing the populace to keep up Hallowe'en much as in the past; and the midwinter solstice, the Scandinavian Yule, was adopted as the feast day of Christ Himself. The continuity of tradition thus made plain, ordinary folk were able to accept the new religion without doing violence to their conscience.

From the point of view of the villager, the multiplicity of saints' days which developed during the Middle Ages was providential. The first sense of the word 'holiday' is 'holy day', and 'holy days' were the only 'holidays' a peasant was likely to get. He naturally approved of the saints. 'Merry England' was merry to the extent that the common people transferred to the saints' days the festivities formerly associated with a pagan calendar and had a vested interest in ensuring that they were not forgotten.

The incentive becomes obvious if we examine many of the old customs that have survived to the present day or to the nineteenth century. We shall find that they have one common feature. They were made an excuse for asking for alms!

Thus the Christmas mumming plays almost always included in the cast a character bearing some such name as 'Little Johnny Jack', a tatterdemalion who shuffled on to the stage clad in rags and having a batch of rag dolls pinned to his shabby overcoat.

> Here comes I, little Johnny Jack,
> With my wife and my children at my back.
> Out of eleven I have but seven,
> And three of them are gone to Heaven.
> One to the Workhouse he is gone,
> And the rest will go when I get home ...

Another character is Father Christmas, who acts as compère and who from time to time addresses "the beloved company" – the audience before whom they are performing, which means the squire at "the big house" and his guests. At the end of the play comes the appeal, delivered sometimes by Father Christmas, sometimes by Little Johnny Jack.

> Christmas comes but once a year,
> And when it comes it brings good cheer.
> Roast beef, plum pudding and mince pie,
> Who likes that better than Father Christmas and I?
> Each one of them is a very good thing,
> And a pot of your Christmas ale will make our
> voices ring!

With the development of modern folklore, we have learned to value the survivals from the remote past which the mumming plays and similar rural dramas and customs represent, but they owe nothing to previous generations of the literary élite who, with the exception of Shakespeare, tended to regard such rustic effusions as beneath their contempt. The participants for their part clung tenaciously to a tradition with such valuable perquisites.

The same theme runs through the whole cycle of rural festivals.

> Christmas is coming, and the geese are getting fat,
> Please to put a penny in the old man's hat.

> "Penny for the guy, mister." (Guy Fawkes' Day)

> The first of May is Garland Day,
> So please remember the garland;
> We don't come here but once a year
> So please remember the garland.

This was chanted by children who knocked at doors and invited the householders to admire the garlands they had made and to contribute a penny or so.

On Shrove Tuesday children went 'a-Shroving' ...

> Please, ma'am, I've come a-shroving,
> For a piece of pancake,
> Or a little chuckle cheese
> Of your own making ...

St Catherine and St Clement have their official festivals near each other in November (25th and 23rd respectively), so the two were coupled in the following begging song, recorded for Sussex:

Cattern and Clemen be here, here, here,
Give us your apples and give us your beer ...
Give us your best
And not your worst,
And God give your soul good rest.

21st December, the shortest day of the year, is St Thomas's Day, also known as 'Mumping Day' ('to mump' meaning to beg) or as 'Gooding Day'. Until towards the end of the nineteenth century, 'going gooding' was a well-established custom and was indulged in by people who were reasonably well off and would not have thought of begging at any other time. In particular, the poor expected tradesmen to give them presents on that day and were not slow in reminding them.

In general the frequent demands for alms were accepted with tolerance, but one custom which met with some opposition was that of Church Ales. These were parish feasts, held in some places at Christmas, in others at Easter or on a saint's day. The main ingredients were "a good plain dinner and plenty of strong beer". The custom was kept up with enthusiasm by most of the parishioners but vigorously opposed by the person who was supposed to provide the drink and victuals, who was in some instances the parson and in some the parish clerk. However, the conflict of interests was possible of solution, for in some parishes the traditional supplier was recompensed by each guest making him a present. He sometimes made a very good thing out of it. In fact, there is an eighteenth-century instance, from Ogbourne St George, in Wiltshire, of an old cripple (a peasant with a small herd of cows) cashing in on the idea for his own benefit. "He had a herd's ale every year. He used to have a barrel of beer and victuals, and people used to drink and give him what they chose."

The mediaeval parson was in the parish and of the parish but not always beloved by the parish. It depended on local circumstances. Where friction existed between the lord of the manor and the villagers, on whose side was he? Obviously his relationship with the lord was different from that of the peasant, and yet here he was, living in the village rather than in the big house and so much more vulnerable to any attempt to work off grievances. The parson had his own fields, his own rights on the common, and his own barns in which he stored the tithes (every tenth sheaf) which he collected from his resentful neighbours at harvest-time. It was not an enviable position for the poor man, but the arrangement persisted for many a century. Sometimes the parson frankly took the side of the lord; sometimes he held the office as a sinecure, living elsewhere and delegating his duties to an ill-paid curate; sometimes, in years of war or pestilence, the priest's house remained vacant for long periods; but sometimes an honest and humble priest spent a lifetime serving God in one parish and was greatly loved by his parishioners.

The church, the priest and the old customs now associated with the Christian rather than the pagan calendar thus loomed large in the lives of mediaeval villagers. Their role in the physical shaping of the countryside may have been incidental, but their influence is still strong in the annual cycle of rural life in the twentieth century. The activities of the Church at the higher levels was, however, far from incidental. For the mediaeval Church was one of the great landowners of the country, probably the greatest after the king.

Just as the lowly parish priest lived side by side with his flock, so the bishop and archbishop were required to live, on more or less level terms, with the local magnates and with the king. They were recruited largely from noble families and were suitably endowed with lands. The church militant was a familiar phenomenon in the mediaeval scene.

The monasteries were, as befitted their original inspiration, something apart from the ordinary paths of life. The monastic ideal began, in the dark years of the break-up of the Roman Empire, with men protesting against and withdrawing from the wicked world. They retired to remote places in desert or wilderness, at first as solitary hermits, then into ascetic communities of like-minded persons. In the chaos of the barbarian invasions, these communities formed oases in which the arts and spirit of civilization were kept alive. In the early monasteries men divided their time between prayer and participation in religious offices and work on the land, in the workshops and in *scriptoria* where manuscripts were patiently copied. The debt that later ages owed to the monasteries is incalculable.

But more settled times brought temptations. Endowed by kings and other great landowners, often no doubt from the same motives which impelled them to build expensive churches and chantries ('fire escapes', they were called by the irreverent, their purpose being to help the donor to escape from hell fire!), the monasteries and abbeys acquired vast estates and all the wealth and luxury which naturally accrued. With these acquisitions came manpower, in the form of serfs, who took over the hard and menial tasks formerly performed by the monks. Reformers like St Bernard of Clairvaux and St Francis of Assisi railed against the decadence of the older orders and instituted new communities which, for a time, held true to their founders' pristine vision but afterwards fell back into the comfortable bog of mediocrity. Long before Henry VIII suppressed the monasteries, the monks in England had made themselves thoroughly unpopular, not so much because of what they did but because of what they did not do. In a frugal and hard-working society, they stood out as lazy and useless parasites.

A notable exception to the general disapproval of monastic establishments was to be found in the dales of Yorkshire. Here, during the reigns of the Norman kings, Cistercian monks from France founded new abbeys (in a region despoiled and depopulated by William the Conqueror in his 'harrying of the North' in 1069-70) which brought back into the sphere of agricultural production huge areas of empty land. In particular they fostered the development of sheep farming, on which the wealth of mediaeval England came to be founded.

The role of the monasteries in mediaeval England is complex, and the motives of their rulers even more so. On the one hand, their achievement in keeping alive the flame of civilization during the Dark Ages was due largely to their isolation from outside events. Inside the monastery walls a cloistered calm prevailed. Yet that same comparative immunity from outside influences tended to make the inmates ultra-conservative and reactionary. They were often unaware of changes and new ideas sweeping through the world outside. Far from being in the forefront in the abolition of serfdom (slavery thinly disguised), the abbeys and monasteries dragged their feet. Employing the age-old arguments of insensitive men who will perform for the Church deeds which they would be ashamed of admitting for their own profit, they resisted attempts by enlightened abbots to free the serfs by manumission, on the grounds that no individual had the power to alienate the property (i.e. the serfs) of the Church. On the other hand, some were sufficiently in touch with secular events to take advantage of them. The growth of the English wool industry owed much to the example and pioneer work of the great abbeys. The achievements of the Yorkshire abbeys in reclaiming extensive areas of waste land was duplicated elsewhere, as in the Fens and in Somerset, where much marsh land was drained and cultivated.

The abbeys and monasteries farmed extensively on their own account. A census of livestock owned by the Abbey of Glastonbury in 1252 lists 892 oxen, 60 bullocks, 23 colts, 223 cows, 19 bulls, 153 heifers and young oxen, 26 steers, 126 yearlings, 6,717 sheep and 327 pigs. The size of the sheep flock is impressive.

Little is known about what crops were cultivated behind monastery walls, but it seems certain that to generations of mediaeval monastic gardeners we are indebted for many of our familiar vegetables, herbs, fruits and flowers. Fifteenth-century documents mention cabbage, onion, turnip, parsnip, radish, leek, parsley, beetroot, carrot, colewort and a number of herbs. In the flower garden were several varieties of rose, lilies and many wild plants brought into the garden, such as cowslips, primroses, violets and periwinkles. Apples, pears, cherries and 'nuts' (probably cob nuts or walnuts) were grown in orchards, and in the late fourteenth century Chaucer was able to mention at least five varieties of apple. Warden pears, highly popular in late mediaeval times, were introduced by the Cistercians in the reign of Edward I. Vineyards were not uncommon in southern England in late Saxon times but later diminished in number, largely through competition with the vineyards of Gascony, from which wine was a major import during the centuries when Gascony and England were under the same crown. On the farms, flax, being needed for linen clothes, was grown much more extensively than today. Two other crops now little known were woad and madder, grown for producing material for dyes.

In suitable country most ecclesiastical and many secular establishments had fishponds, well stocked with carp, eel, perch and other species, for which the demand on Fridays and in Lent would have been very great. Fish-weirs were constructed at intervals along the major rivers and trapped large quantities of eels as well as salmon and lampreys. The latter, now little valued, were a highly-prized gourmet dish in the Middle Ages.

Mediaeval visitors to England noted the abundance of wild game, using the term in its broadest sense. Every creature with enough flesh on its bones, from a sparrow upwards, was eaten. In the fourteenth century ten finches could be bought for a penny. Other birds featuring in the mediaeval bill of fare included thrushes, larks, hawks and the decidedly fishy herons, bitterns and swans. The knowledge of rural methods of netting and snaring small birds lingered to within the range of living memory. Wherever sufficient areas of water existed, decoy ponds for snaring waterfowl were constructed. Examples of these, and of monastic fishponds, still survive.

An essential personage in the life of a mediaeval village was the miller. In early times grain was slowly ground by hand with a quern, a method which was still employed in Wales until about the tenth century. In common with other Middle Eastern and Mediterranean empires, the Romans used mills in which heavy stones were turned by slaves harnessed to a capstan-like device. After the abolition of slavery, horses or donkeys replaced slaves for this purpose, but water-mills, probably invented by the Romans, were introduced to Britain during the late Roman period. Water-mills continued to operate after the Saxon invasion and indeed came into widespread use. At the time of the Domesday Book there were at least five thousand water-mills in England.

As a rule, each manor had its own water-mill, to which all the peasants on the manor had to bring their corn for grinding. As they had to pay a toll for each sack, the monopoly was a valuable one, and in many places energetic steps were taken to prevent peasants from using their own private querns. Later the miller, formerly an employee of the lord of the manor, leased out the milling rights for a cash rent. The unpopularity of the system was then transferred to the miller, who was widely accused of sharp practice.

> Miller-dee, miller-dee, dusty poll,
> How many sacks of flour hast thou stole?
> In goes a bushel; out comes a peck;
> Hang old miller-dee up by the neck!

Early in the Middle Ages, a new type of mill was introduced, the windmill. The first record of one in England is dated 1191, and a century later they were common, especially in districts where water-mills were not practicable.

Two important features of the mediaeval centuries had a tremendous impact on life in our islands. One was a deterioration in the climate, the other the occurrence of widespread pestilence, notably the Black Death. The two are linked.

The age of the migration of nations, which spilled the barbarians into the West, was characterized by mild, dry weather. The Anglo-Saxons and later the Vikings took advantage of these conditions to voyage over the northern seas, the latter reaching and colonizing both Iceland and Greenland, and the Vikings pushing on to the American mainland. After about 800 the climate began to deteriorate. Cold and dry spells alternated, but the outstanding characteristic of the weather throughout the Middle Ages was storminess. Contemporary records show, for instance, that every year from 1086 to 1100 was marked by storms and floods. In 1091, 1092, 1093, 1099 and 1100, there were severe inundations along the east coast, especially in spring, and in 1092 large estates in Kent belonging to Earl Godwin were submerged, to form the Goodwin Sands. In 1098 *The Anglo-Saxon Chronicle* records, "the great rains ceased not all the year".

In the middle of the thirteenth century the pendulum swung towards drought and heat. 1252 and 1253 were severely affected by drought. In 1252 no rain fell in April, May, June and July; in 1253 many mill-streams dried up, making the grinding of corn impossible. In 1310 a cycle of wet summers began, giving rise to serious famines in 1313–17. More bad weather followed in 1339–42, with resultant famine, which was felt more severely in Scotland than in England. And so to 1348, when a bad harvest in the previous year was followed by the first appearance of the Black Death.

The unsettled period lasted until about 1376, when a series of abundant harvests began, setting the pattern for much of the fifteenth century. 'Famine years' occurred more frequently in the sixteenth century, though until the middle of the century good harvests were in the majority. Thereafter the climate deteriorated again, with heavy storms in summer and increasingly severe winters. The polar character of the winters of the first half of the seventeenth century is illustrated by the frequency of Frost Fairs on the frozen Thames in London.

About midsummer in 1348 the Black Death was brought by ship to Melcombe Regis in Dorset. In the next two years it spread to the remotest parts of England, Wales, Scotland and Ireland, and when at last its force was spent, approximately one-third of the population had perished. Philip Ziegler, who has studied the available data carefully, estimates in his book *The Black Death* that the total death toll was probably about 1,400,000.

Although the plague originated in the East and was spread by the fleas which infested the black rat, there can be little doubt that its spread must have been assisted by the lack of hygiene in mediaeval villages and towns and by the low resistance of much of the populace, due to inadequate nutrition. Famine and pestilence have always been intimately connected. By the time of the Black Death, Britain had become overpopulated for the contemporary system of farming. There could have been few villages in which the open-field system had not been in operation for at least four or five hundred years, and although livestock were allowed to graze over each field in its fallow year, their contribution towards the replenishment of the fertility of the soil must have been very inadequate. In short, the soil was becoming exhausted. In the meantime, with the pressure of increasing population, the villagers had been encroaching steadily on the encircling zone of 'waste' around their parish, until now in many instances their fields adjoined those of their neighbours in the next parish. In some districts wood had become so scarce that peasants were using cowdung for fuel, with consequent further deprivation of the soil. Animals were naturally feeling the pinch. With them, too, lack of nutrition made them an easy prey to disease, and the records of the thirteenth and fourteenth centuries contain an increasing number of references to 'murrain', which includes a wide diversity of ailments. Some chroniclers seem to suggest that the Black Death itself took its toll of cattle, sheep, pigs, dogs and even poultry, though whether this was so or whether they fell victim to some similar epidemic we cannot say. Great numbers must have perished from sheer neglect at the time of the Black Death, for a contemporary record mentions that "sheep and cattle roamed about, wandering in fields and through the growing harvest, and there was no one to drive them off or collect them, but in ditches and thickets they died in innumerable quantities in every part for lack of guardians, for so great a dearth of servants and labourers existed that no one knew what to do".

Recent students, making detailed analyses of estate rolls and similar documents, have concluded that, before the plague, the country was suffering from a surplus of labour. There seem to have been, say, two or three men available for every one man's job. By the same reckoning, two or three men would have to share one man's subsistence. The Black Death could be said to have relieved a situation that was becoming intolerable.

The Black Death did not fade away gradually, like a retreating comet. For the rest of the century it flared up again frequently. The main recrudescences occurred in 1361, 1368–9, 1371, 1375, 1390 and 1405. Some of these, notably that of 1361, were almost as catastrophic as the first visitation, and in each instance the toll of the new generation was heavy.

Obviously things would never be the same again, but as recovery began, after 1349, the landowners tried to restore the *status quo*. Attempts were made, and reinforced by new laws, to compel peasants, labourers and others of the lower classes to resume their customary obligations to their superiors. It was a thankless task, on the whole, for in many places no one of any stratum of society was left alive to say what the ancient rights and duties were. Death was not the only problem; in the confusion innumerable men wandered away from their birthplaces to better themselves by offering to work elsewhere for a cash wage. Plenty of desperate manors were to be found who would employ them with no questions asked. In short, the working classes discovered the advantages attached to freedom of movement. The feudal system was dying.

For once in the history of our islands, land was more plentiful than the labour to work it. There was therefore an increased incentive to turn to a style of farming which required little labour, namely, sheep farming. With the development of a profitable trade in wool and woollen cloth, more and more landowners had already enclosed considerable sections of their domains as sheep-walks, to the alarm and protests of their resident peasants, who saw their rights on former common land thus disappearing. Now the trend was accelerated.

The reasons for the obliteration of mediaeval villages from the map are complex. Suffice to say here that an impressive number of villages did so disappear in the Middle Ages. A recent survey by Maurice Beresford and John G. Hurst, in their book *Deserted Mediaeval Villages*, catalogues no fewer than 2,263 of which the sites are approximately known. This is in England alone, and the list is by no means complete. A Deserted Mediaeval Village Research Group is busily collecting data about more. It is true to say, though, that many villages were entirely depopulated and never rebuilt at the time of the Black Death. And also that the creation of great sheep-walks, albeit through lack of any alternative use for the land, was a powerful contributory factor.

It seems that the population did not recover sufficiently to exert any pressure on rural resources until the 1480s. From that time onwards, we read of vigorous protests against the enclosures of land for sheep-walks and the alleged dispossession of peasants in consequence. But John Hales, writing in 1549, rightly recorded that "the chief destruction of towns [meaning townships or villages] and decay of houses was before the beginning of the reign of King Henry VII [1485]".

The face of the countryside was thus radically changed in these mediaeval centuries. And it has been said that the most plentiful earthworks in England today are those which mark the sites of abandoned mediaeval villages.

6

The Age of Improvement

The old open-field system had, despite its theoretical excellence, demonstrated its weaknesses. It failed to take full account of human nature. A man will care for his own garden plot, digging in manure, eradicating weeds and generally improving it so that as the years go by its fertility is increased rather than diminished, but where is the point of taking all that trouble one year if the next year the land will belong to a feckless neighbour? So the idea of an annual transfer of plots in the open fields, splendid though it would seem to be both logically and ethically, foundered on that practical consideration.

The term 'The Age of Enclosures' is generally applied to the eighteenth and early nineteenth centuries, but, as already noted, enclosures were becoming common in mediaeval times. Enclosures to enlarge the lord's private domain, enclosures of common land, enclosures of vast areas of grazing land for sheep-farming, even enclosures of sections of forest, all were in progress during the later Middle Ages. In the years after the Black Death, there was so much land to be cultivated by so few workers that there were few objections to any type of enclosure.

From early times the lord of the manor had commonly reserved for his own use not only baulks in the open fields but also a block of land around his castle or manor house. When sheep farming became profitable through the development of the wool trade, this 'home farm' was likely to be enclosed and devoted entirely to pasture for the sheep. As opportunity or need arose, the domain would be added to by further enclosures. And, with the changing years, the work on the lord's domain would be done less and less by peasants performing their feudal service and more and more by paid labourers.

Came the time when, by inclination or necessity, the lord of the manor no longer wanted to cultivate his home domain. One cogent factor was the soaring price of labour after the Black Death, which in general doubled in a single year and thereafter continued to increase. The way out was to let the land to an ambitious and reasonably prosperous peasant. The lord of the manor thus became a landlord, deriving much of his income from rents, while the peasant took a big step up the social ladder. Like the lord of the manor, he now had not only his strips of land in the open fields but also a compact group of fields, with buildings, which he could improve in the knowledge that he would benefit from his efforts. Long leases, even for life, gradually became the custom. The peasant had become a tenant farmer, a 'franklin', who, as we learn from Chaucer, could be a very prosperous individual indeed. By the late fifteenth century it was possible for a yeoman farmer's son, Hugh Latimer, to become a bishop. Hugh Latimer senior held two hundred acres as a tenant and owned a hundred sheep and thirty milking cows.

Nevertheless, the open-field system continued predominant over much of the country until well into the eighteenth century. Enclosures of common lands tended to meet with increasing local resistance after the middle of the fifteenth century, when the population had substantially recovered from the effects of the Black Death. Moreover, by ancient law, a lord seeking to enclose any part of his manor, all of which theoretically belonged to him, had to leave enough common land to enable a cottager to get his living from the rights he enjoyed there, coupled with his holdings in the open fields.

Also, with the object lesson of the private farms on their doorstep, progressive peasants with holdings in the open fields set about demonstrating that the old system was not entirely impervious to progress. In fact, it proved more flexible than was at one time imagined. Basically, it was pedantically democratic, in that no variation, for instance, in the traditional cropping rotation of the open fields was permissible without the consent of every peasant with rights there. To adapt to the changing circumstances, however, majority decisions became acceptable, thus making it possible to set aside unreasonable opposition by a few diehards.

By the seventeenth century the cropping of the open fields was beginning to show considerable diversification. One of the earliest innovations was to sow part of each big arable field to a grass ley, either for grazing or for hay. This division cut right across the individual strips, though each householder was required to contribute a proportion of his holding in return for a share in the use of the grass. It is uncertain whether the leys were sown under a cereal crop or not. In the second half of the seventeenth century sainfoin was introduced to England and soon achieved popularity. How it fitted into the system is illustrated by the arrangement worked out at Taston, near Woodstock, Oxfordshire. In one of the open fields, five furlongs were set aside in the year 1700 for growing sainfoin, but apparently each individual who had a claim to a part of those five furlongs (and there were twenty-two of them) had to sow the sainfoin seed on his own section. The sainfoin was cut for hay, each farmer taking what grew on his own land. Then cows were allowed in to graze, on the basis of two cows for each yardland (about forty acres) held in the parish. After 13th October sheep too were allowed in to graze, on the basis of six mature sheep and ten lambs per yardland. Grazing was permitted till 2nd January, when all animals were turned off, to allow the sainfoin to recover. Growing fodder crops in the open fields in this way was known as 'hitching'. Other leguminous crops, such as peas, beans, vetches and red clover, were also soon taking their place in a rotation which grew more and more complex.

Simultaneously a 'rationalization' of the old system of allocating strips in the open fields annually was proceeding. It took two forms. First, the annual share-out of land became difficult as the cropping plan grew more complicated, so there was a tendency to allow the tenancies for the various strips to persist year after year. Secondly, individual tenants tried to get hold of adjoining strips which could be welded into a compact field. Enterprising and ambitious peasants could thus acquire a much more viable though still fragmented farm. In time they would be able, on the pretext of preventing their livestock from straying, to erect fences or hedges around their lands, thus consolidating their hold on them.

Whether or not the change was socially desirable, it certainly made for more efficient husbandry, both with crops and with livestock. Under the old system each manor had a common herd of cattle and flock of sheep, under the care of the appropriate expert, though the animals belonged to individual owners. The arrangement is described by Thomas Davis, of Longleat, who undertook an agricultural survey of Wiltshire for the recently-formed Board of Agriculture in 1811.

Cow commons ... were more numerous formerly, many of them having been converted at different times into sheep downs by consent of the commoners ... The common herd of cows begin to feed the cow downs early in May, usually Holyrood-day, and finished when the fields are clear of corn. At the beginning and end of the season they are driven to the down in the morning and brought back in the evening; but in the heat of summer they are only kept on the down during the night, and in the morning they are brought back into the villages, where they feed on the lanes and small marshes by the riverside, if such there be, till after the evening milking. When the stubble-fields are open, the cows have a right to feed them jointly with the sheep, and if there are common meadows, they have an exclusive right to feed them till the end of the commoning season, usually St Martin's Day, November 11th, when the owners take them home to the straw-yards. The cow down, when the cows leave it to go to the stubble-fields, becomes common for the sheep flock during all or a certain part of the winter, when it is again laid up for the cows.

As for the sheep.

The common sheep down is open for the common flocks during the summer and autumn. The unsown or summer field is also open till it is ploughed for wheat; after that, the sheep have only the down till the harvest is over. When the corn fields are clear, the flock has those fields and the down till the winter obliges the owners to give them hay. Until this period, they are folded on the arable fields in a common fold; but when they begin to eat hay, every commoner finds his own fold and his own hay, the common shepherd feeding and folding the whole.

Davis comments that, although that was the ancient custom of managing sheep, "latterly the tenants of common fields have introduced the practice of folding their separate flocks on their own lands, thereby placing their sheep under the immediate care of their own servants, rather than entrusting them to a common shepherd, whose neglect or partiality made his attentions inadequate to the care of the whole".

It is not surprising that the beginning of the general improvement of livestock and the establishment of modern methods of selective breeding coincided with this change of practice.

The Board of Agriculture, for which Thomas Davis's survey, quoted above, was prepared, was established in 1793. The reports which it promptly commissioned on the agriculture of the respective counties ought to have given the fullest accounts of the rural economy since the Domesday Book. They are, in fact, extremely one-sided and biased. By analysing the entries in the Domesday Book, we can form a fairly well-balanced picture of England both before and after the Norman Conquest. By studying the surveys for the Board of Agriculture, we learn a great deal about the new styles of farming on enclosed land but very little about the old system which they replaced. As an example, the Reverend Arthur Young, having written 472 pages of his *General View of the Agriculture of the County of Sussex*, devotes one sentence to the pre-enclosure set-up, under the heading of "Obstacles to Improvement", as follows:

Common Rights

These are unexceptionably the most perfect nuisance that ever blasted the improvement of a country; and till they are done away with, no tolerable husbandry will flourish in those districts where they are in force.

The Reports were, of course, written for a self-satisfied and arrogant ruling class to whom the independence of the peasants, fostered by the old system, was an affront and, as Young put it, an obstacle. In fact, it was, as the compiler of the *Report on Shropshire* expressed it, an obstacle to "that subordination of the lower ranks of society which in the present times is so much wanted". "The use of common land by labourers," said the writer, "operates upon the mind as a sort of independence." Let it be abolished and "the labourers will work every day of the year, and their children will be put out to labour early".

Much the same sentiments were expressed by John Billingsley, who prepared the *Report on Somerset* for the Board in 1795. His opinion was,

> The possession of a cow or two, with a hog and a few geese, naturally exalts a peasant, in his own conception, above his brethren in the same rank of society. It inspires some degree of confidence in a property, inadequate to his support. In sauntering after his cattle, he acquires a habit of indolence. Quarter, half and occasionally whole days are imperceptibly lost. Day labour becomes disgusting; the aversion increases indulgence; and at length the sale of a half-fed calf or hog furnishes the means of adding intemperance to idleness.

The class for whom Billingsley was writing was busily rectifying this state of affairs. For them it was not difficult. All that was needed was a private member's bill before Parliament. And Parliament consisted exclusively of large landowners; indeed, one could not become a member of Parliament unless one had a considerable acreage of land. Moreover, the enclosure bills became so numerous that they were passed to committees to deal with, and these committees consisted, according to Parliamentary investigation in 1825, of "members who have been most interested in the result".

The general principle behind the Enclosure Acts would seem to be equitable. Each householder with rights in a parish, or on the land proposed for enclosure, was required to set down those rights in writing. His claim properly established, the land was divided out among the claimants in proportion to their former rights. In practice it was far from satisfactory. Many an illiterate peasant must have found the task of writing out his claim completely beyond him. Even supposing he managed to get the task done for him, an unsympathetic and unscrupulous lawyer employed by the landowner who was introducing the bill could usually find technical loopholes.

The division of the land according to the rights previously enjoyed ensured that the landowner had the lion's share. Nor was there anything in law to require an equitable division according to the quality of the land. A peasant with rights that

Stone, brick, tiles and wood, the traditional materials of medieval building, used to make the cross, smithy and church at Lund, North Humberside.

The Age of Faith. *Above:* Church tithes would be collected at this fourteenth-century tithe barn at Bredon, Worcestershire. *Left:* The tower of the Saxon church (*c.*1000) at Earls Barton, Northamptonshire.

Above: A thirteenth-century tithe barn at Great Coxwell, Oxford-shire. *Below:* A long house, *c.*1600 or earlier, at Ollsbrim, near Dartmeet, Devonshire.

Pyecombe forge, Sussex, operated continuously (apart from a brief period in this century) from the days of Charles II until the death of the last blacksmith, Sean Black, in 1976.

Field boundaries, walled and hedged. *Above:* Eighteenth-century boundaries, with walled access lanes, at Malham, West Yorkshire. *Below:* Fields near Bishop's Castle, Shropshire, seen from the Long Mynd.

Above: A post-enclosure group of farm buildings, Gally Gap Farm, near Howsham on the western edge of the Wolds. *Below:* The Rhine, near Glastonbury in the Vale of Avalon, Somerset – such watercourses are wide and deep enough to act as field boundaries.

The Leeds and Liverpool Canal at Skipton, which it reached in 1773.

eventually entitled him to, say, two acres of land in the share-out, might well find that his two acres were on a thorny hillside a mile or two from the village. Then, too, there were the legal costs to be met. In practice, the smaller claimants often had to sell their modest plots of land to the landowner in order to raise the necessary cash.

The flagrant manipulation of power to achieve the desired results and the abuses which occurred are ably described by J.L. and Barbara Hammond in their classic *The Village Labourer*. Enclosing was, to those who promoted the bills, frankly a way of enlarging their estates and in many instances a means of obtaining more collateral for raising loans to pay their debts. The bills were pushed through with single-mindedness and determination. As previously noted, enclosures were proceeding during the Middle Ages, and in the late fifteenth and sixteenth centuries were arousing stiff opposition. The Civil War and other troubles of the seventeenth century took men's minds off the subject, to some extent, but in the eighteenth century the landowning classes returned to it with renewed interest. As the Jacobite controversy receded and a Hanoverian peace prevailed, men turned their attention to domestic affairs, and great rural estates became fashionable. Between 1702 and 1762 Parliament passed 246 private enclosure acts, covering some 400,000 acres. But before the end of the century a further two thousand Acts had been processed, involving more than three million acres. And in the first forty or so years of the nineteenth century another two thousand Acts dealt with a further two and a half million acres. The bulk of these Acts referred to the Midlands, southern and eastern England, as far north as and including Yorkshire. Professor G.M. Trevelyan, in *English Social History*, explains that in Kent, Essex and Sussex much of the acreage had already been enclosed, while in the west and north the moorlands were so extensive and poor as to be of little interest to enclosers. So the six million or so acres of land enclosed between 1700 and about 1845 were confined to about half the counties of England, a concentration which meant that in some counties the greater part of the farmland was involved. The enclosure fever hit Scotland as energetically as England and with equally drastic effects, for there were even fewer restrictions on

Scottish lairds than on English landlords. Wales was not so extensively affected, largely because, in that land of sheep and cattle pastures, most cultivated land was already enclosed.

Immense areas of the countryside thus delivered into their hands, the estate-owners set about transforming the face of Britain. It is largely to them that we are indebted for the now familiar rural scene. The pre-enclosure countryside would today strike us as strange and even foreign, more akin to the open, hedgeless fields of the northern European plain than to the tamed and cosy scenery we now associate with rural England. Over much of England and Scotland the present network of fields was established, the very farm and estate boundaries mapped out, country mansions built, woods planted, lakes formed and innumerable minor and often bizarre features created by landowners developing their newly-won properties.

One of the first actions of a landowner after an enclosure act was to obliterate the old open fields and to divide them up into rectangular fields of convenient size (which varied according to district and location but was usually between five and thirty acres). Each field was fenced with a hedge, generally of hawthorn, which was frequently termed 'quickset' because it took root and grew rapidly. Permanent tracks or droves were laid out for access but were not usually surfaced. In many instances surviving award maps and the attached schedules illustrate exactly what happened in a particular locality.

Incidentally, in 1838 tithe was commuted from a payment in kind to a cash payment, and an assessment or rating made for each unit of land. In parishes where the two have survived, it is interesting to compare the enclosure award map with the tithe award map. The enclosure award map may, for instance, refer to 1808, and so the 1838 map will reveal what houses were built or demolished and what changes in field boundaries occurred in the intervening thirty years. A fascinating aspect of the study is to note how field names moved about over the map. For example, a marshy hollow would in Old English parlance be termed a 'plash', and the name occurs on a number of enclosure maps. But twenty or thirty years later, 'Plash Field' may appear as a name given to a large field with a marshy bottom along one side of it. Acreages, too, become confused. On land which I used to farm is a field known as 'Nineacres'. Its actual acreage is fifteen. Men of a generation previous to my own told me they could remember when it was divided by hedges into a number of small fields of one to two acres each. Evidently at some time an owner managed to get possession of enough of them to form a field of nine acres and so, with a typical lack of imagination, called it Nineacres. Later another six acres were added to the field, but the name stuck.

The big country landowners of the eighteenth and early nineteenth centuries were great foresters, and we owe them a debt for replanting and preserving much of the deciduous forests of England. They had a strong motive, apart from the fashion for impressive landscape planning. The height of the enclosure movement coincided (though it was not mere coincidence) with the wars against France. Enormous quantities of mature oaks were felled to make "the wooden walls of England", and patriotic landowners considered it their duty to ensure a future supply of trees for the same purpose. Indeed, the despoliation of Britain's forests was well advanced even before the Napoleonic Wars started. In the New Forest a survey, commissioned by James I, indicated that in 1608 there were 123,927 oak trees with timber fit for the Navy. A similar survey in 1783 showed that the number of oaks had dwindled to 12,447. Within the space of 170 years or so the Forest had been decimated. At about the same period, the oaks of the valleys and glens of Scotland were being felled with a complete disregard of the future, changing the face of the Scottish countryside permanently.

A favourite type of woodland with the rural estate-owner was the open deciduous coppice. In it, oaks, beeches and a few other species were fairly thinly spaced to allow for a vigorous growth of underwood, notably hazel but in some districts chestnut or ash. A system of broad rides was carefully planned to allow stands for the guns when pheasant-shooting. The underwood was cut at regular intervals, generally about eight years. It was usually sold, standing, to independent village craftsmen who spent the winter cutting it and making it into hurdles, sheep-cribs, tool handles, thatching spars and other useful articles. Thus it played an important part in the rural economy, providing, incidentally, a living for many peasants who had lost their common rights.

When preparing a plan for his newly-acquired lands the estate-owner bore in mind the requirements for sport in the arable fields. There shelter-belts of trees were planted, largely to harbour pheasants but in some instances to make driven partridges rise, so that they would offer satisfactory targets to guns stationed on the far side. The earlier shelter-belts were often of beech or mixed woods, but the later ones frequently of spruce or pine, these conifers being little known in southern England before that time. John Aubrey, the first historian of Wiltshire, who wrote in the middle of the seventeenth century, states categorically that beeches were also an innovation and that the only ones he knew in the county were some in Grovely Wood. If his observation was sound, the appearance of the chalk hills of southern England without their familiar beech clumps must have been very different from what it is today.

The rounded beech clumps that are now such prominent features of the chalk hill summits are certainly the product of imaginative landscape planning. Quite frequently they were planted on or around ancient hill-top earthworks. A quaint fancy by an early-nineteenth-century landowner may be seen near Amesbury, Wiltshire, where a galaxy of small round clumps of trees represents the battle plan of the British and French fleets just before the Battle of Trafalgar, each clump marking the position of a ship. They are known locally as the Trafalgar Clumps. Some have been destroyed in recent years to make way for the A 303 highway bypassing Amesbury.

The fashionable and ideal nucleus for a great estate of the age of enclosure was a vast and impressive mansion set in formal gardens and surrounded by a spacious park. Important accessory features were a lake and follies. The latter might be imposing monuments set on a hill or an ornate, mock-Grecian temple or a figure carved in the turf of a hillside. Most of the white horses and other figures that adorn chalk hills in southern England are follies of this date. Great houses had, of course, been a common feature of the English countryside for many a century. They were the direct descendants of the Norman castle and mediaeval manor house, though some had been taken over more or less intact from monastic establishments in the reign of Henry VIII. Now, however, they experienced a breath-taking efflorescence. Planned by the best architects of the day, their interiors designed by the best decorators and artists, equipped by the masterpieces of the golden age of furniture-making, adorned by priceless paintings and by antiques gleaned from almost every corner of the globe, these palaces became veritable treasure-houses.

They remain so, and many are now open for all who can afford the price of admission to inspect, as the descendants of their builders attempt to cope with the financial pressures of the twentieth century. So the pendulum swings to its extremes, for many of the estate-consolidators of the enclosure age seem to have had an almost morbid aversion from association with those whom they considered their social inferiors. When the sixth Duke of Somerset went out in his carriage from his mansion at Petworth, Sussex, he sent his servants in advance to clear the roads of any yokels, lest the vulgar should look on his august personage. When the meditations of the eccentric William Beckford (who inherited a fortune of £100,000 a year from slave-run sugar estates in the West Indies) were disturbed by some horsemen and hounds as he walked through his park, he forthwith ordered the building of a twelve-foot-high wall around the entire estate, a circumference of many miles. Many a village was uprooted and rebuilt on a new site either to make room for the estate-owner's grandiose ideas for his house and park or to satisfy his yearning for isolation. As an example, at Everley, Wiltshire, the estate-owner, Francis Astley, demolished the old village, turned the site into a park and rebuilt the cottages outside the precinct wall. He even secured a special dispensation from the Bishop of Salisbury to pull down the fourteenth-century church and build a new one, on the grounds that the old one was dilapidated and in an inconvenient situation.

There was a complete ruthlessness about these proceedings. At Ilchester, Somerset, in 1819, 163 men, women and children were turned out of their homes in the depth of winter and forced to take refuge in a temporary shelter made of hurdles and straw, many later being driven to look for refuge in the county gaol. This particular instance was so flagrant that it was raised in the House of Commons but was rejected on the grounds that "every man was at liberty to do what he chose with his own property". Much the same was happening in the notorious Highland Clearances, which depopulated so many Scottish estates. Nor was the cavalier attitude of the landowners confined to people. Near Tisbury, Wiltshire, an eighteenth-century Lord Arundell decided that the ruins of Old Wardour Castle, blown up in the Civil War, needed embellishing to make them a congenial picnic spot for his guests on summer afternoons. So he laid out lawns by the lake, planted cedar trees and planned an ornamental grotto. The building material for the grotto consisted of immense stones from a prehistoric monument, said by contemporary writers to have resembled Stonehenge, which was standing in an earthwork a few miles away. His lordship completely dismantled it, so that no one now knows exactly where it stood, but the stones may still be seen in his pleasure-garden by the lake. It seems that Stonehenge was lucky to escape.

Viewed in perspective and without excusing any of the excesses, the altogether drastic reshaping of the countryside was probably necessary. Or let us say that without it the history of Britain would have developed very differently. Let us consider what happened to the dispossessed peasants.

The first and most obvious course was to stay put. Those who came out of the apportionment with sufficient land to make a viable holding continued to farm in most instances. They had the opportunity to become reasonably prosperous yeoman farmers. The estate-owners who took the lion's share were also disposed to let out their land to tenants. The age when most big landowners themselves engaged in agriculture was yet to come, although in Scotland the lairds did become the owners of large sheep flocks. So, in most English villages, there was room for a small number, say a dozen or so, of tenant farmers. The old tradition whereby each farm or estate tended to be self-sufficient had given way, over the centuries, to specialization, so that now most villages had a blacksmith, a miller, a shoemaker, several carpenters and examples of a number of other trades. Certain districts had local industries. In parts of Somerset certain villages were noted for making sail-cloth and similar fabrics; others for gloves or rope; in Hertfordshire a group of villages specialized in the making of straw hats. There remained the dispossessed cottagers, who had managed to eke out a meagre living from seasonal work, coupled with their common rights. These now felt the pinch worst of all. Their destiny was to become landless labourers, working for a pittance and with little hope for any improvement in their lot.

Not that they accepted with any fatalism or equanimity their diminished status. They had little or no political power, and the chronicles of the time were kept almost exclusively by their opponents, but sufficient records remain to make clear that they bitterly resented the changes and did everything they could to prevent them. Occasionally they could claim a success. The *Annual Register* for 1767 mentions:

On Tuesday evening a great number of farmers were observed going along Pall Mall with cockades in their hats. On enquiring the reason, it appeared they all lived in or near the parish of Stanwell in the county of Middlesex, and they were returning to their wives and families to carry them the agreeable news of a Bill being rejected for inclosing the said common, which if carried into execution might have been the ruin of a great number of families.

Stanwell was sufficiently near London for such action to be taken and to have effect. But even so the triumph of the Stanwell peasants was short-lived. The local lord of the manor had another attempt at an enclosure bill and this time succeeded. A petition by the Duke of Marlborough for enclosing and draining four thousand acres of common land on Otmoor, near Oxford, in 1801 met with armed resistance in the parishes concerned. A second attempt, in 1814, resulted in the officials who went to nail the notices to the church doors being met by "large mobs, armed with every description of offensive weapons, having assembled for the purpose of obstructing the persons who went to affix the Notices, and who were prevented by violence, and threats of immediate death, from approaching the churches". In spite of this, the Act was passed, though it did leave large sections of Otmoor as common land. Unrest simmered for another fifteen years or so and then flared up in a full-scale riot in 1830, when the yeomanry were called out and more than forty rioters arrested.

The alternatives to staying on in one's birthplace and trying to adapt to the new regime was to pack up and test one's luck elsewhere. The new manufacturing towns were an obvious goal. Well into the eighteenth century manufacturing was a village affair. The role of such big towns as existed was to act as markets for goods brought in for distribution. However, since the late Middle Ages there had been increasing exploitation of the country's mineral wealth, notably iron. Iron-mining and smelting were associated primarily with woodland regions, such as the Weald of Kent and Sussex, because of the ready availability of apparently unlimited supplies of timber for making charcoal. Lead-mining on the Mendips and tin in Cornwall were other important mining industries, and by the time of Elizabeth I the manufacture of glass was assuming major importance.

Impossible though it must at one time have seemed, the increasing demand for wood for manufacturing and other purposes slowly but inexorably denuded the country of forests. In the sixteenth and seventeenth centuries there are increasing references to shortage of fuel, as, for instance, to people using furze for cooking and to poor women being charged with stealing wood from hedges. As early as the reign of Elizabeth I much 'sea-coal' was brought to London and other places in the south from the mines of Northumberland and Durham, and this traffic increased during the succeeding centuries. It was not until the Napoleonic Wars, however, that coal began to be employed to any extent in smelting iron. James Watt patented his steam-engine in the year 1769. The industrial revolution was well under way.

At the same time, the second half of the eighteenth century saw an enormous increase in the quantity of raw cotton from British plantations in the West Indies. Up to this time cotton weaving had been a cottage industry, but now new inventions, such as Richard Arkwright's spinning frame, began speedily to transform it into a factory operation. The damp climate of Lancashire having proved eminently suited to the handling of cotton, which came into the port of Liverpool, the Lancashire cotton towns mushroomed. Parallel inventions in the manufacture of woollen cloth triggered the migration from the little weaving towns of the West Country to the dales of Yorkshire. And through it all London flourished and grew exceedingly.

Great numbers of the surplus population of the villages were therefore absorbed by the new towns.

The other outlet for the dispossessed peasant was overseas. Emigration on an important scale began in the early seventeenth century, not only in the form of refugees from religious persecution (as the Pilgrim Fathers) but also in official projects for settling in Virginia and other American colonies. It faltered during the Civil War but was afterwards resumed, though on a relatively small scale till after the Napoleonic Wars. Then it became a flood, shiploads of emigrants pouring into not only America and Canada but Australia and, after 1837, New Zealand. Scotland in particular contributed greatly to the colonization of Canada.

It is legitimate to ask, were the villages really depopulated to the extent implied by these massive migrations to the towns and the colonies? An explanation is to be found in an astonishing explosion in population which occurred in the eighteenth century. In the Middle Ages, as noted, the population of England and Wales tended to rise, when uninterrupted by pestilence, to a peak of around four million. By the end of the seventeenth century it had gradually increased to about five and a half million. But within the next hundred years it had leapt to nine million.

The chief factor in this sudden sprint was, surprisingly, a rapid decline in the death rate, which fell from 33·3 per thousand in about 1730 to 19·98 per thousand in 1810. What we know about lack of hygiene, the prevalence of plague and other maladies, the rudimentary state of medical knowledge, the overcrowding in the towns and the wretched living conditions in the villages, and the general ignorance of the age, would seem to make this a truly remarkable phenomenon, but nevertheless it did occur. It seems to indicate that conditions in earlier ages must have been far worse, a fact which is confirmed by what little specific information is available. Consider, for instance, the household of Sir Stephen Fox, one of the great men of the reign of Charles II, paymaster-general to His Majesty's Forces and Lord of the Treasury. This excellent man had six sons and three daughters, which seem to augur well for his ambition to found a dynasty of landed gentry. But all except one of the daughters predeceased him, most of the sons dying young, thus making it necessary for the old man to marry again at the age of seventy-seven, in order to secure the longed-for family.

Incidentally, he did so successfully, becoming the father of twin sons. But if that was typical of the mortality in the families of the great, what must it have been like among the poor? It has been calculated that in the Middle Ages each married woman needed to produce at least six children in order to maintain a level population.

The towns and the colonies, then, were peopled not be draining the villages of their inhabitants but by a burgeoning increase in population. Indeed, when the emigration movement was at its height, there were still more people in the villages than they knew how to cope with. Old William Cobbett, stumping the country with his muddle-headed but vigorously-expressed economic gospel, was continually railing against the policy of encouraging, by carrot and stick, the rural population to leave their old homes. In particular he inveighs against the then fashionable theories of Malthus, whose philosophy he sums up in the phrase, "that the human race has a natural tendency to increase beyond the means of sustenance for them".

On horseback down the valley of the Salisbury Avon in the summer of 1826 he counted twenty-nine parishes between Pewsey and Salisbury, with a total population of 9,116. He then calculated that these villagers were producing enough food to feed 45,580 persons at a comfortable standard of nutrition, or 136,740 at the subsistence level which they themselves endured. Yet, he storms, "there is an Emigration Committee sitting to devise means of getting rid of these working people, who are grudged even the miserable morsel that they get!"

His contention was that people should live where the food was produced. He visualized a country in which, as the population increased, so the existing villages would expand at more or less equal rates, thus perpetuating a semi-rural populace with its feet firmly on the soil. The idea is an attractive one which, if found practicable and if followed, could well have avoided much misery and have resulted in a better-balanced population than the top-heavy urban one which did develop. But he was too late. Nor is it to be supposed that, even if he had been earlier with his message, he would have had any success in diverting the current of events.

A typical village after an enclosure act consisted of one large estate, with perhaps a few independent farmers owning their own land. There was also a fairly numerous group of smallholders who had been given plots of land, usually of not more than an acre and frequently less, to compensate for the loss of common rights. Legal and other expenses (for instance, in some parishes everyone was required to contribute equally to the cost of fencing the entire area, which meant that the peasant with one acre had to subsidize the man with five hundred acres) swallowed up the majority of these smallholdings, reducing their owners to the status of labourers.

These small-time peasants had been labourers before, eking out their income from the animals grazing on the commons by doing seasonal work for their larger neighbours. Now, however, they found themselves wholly dependent on their wages. As their numbers increased and as war forced up the prices of food and other commodities, so the former rates of wages proved inadequate for subsistence. So in 1795, at Speenhamland in Berkshire, a scheme was worked out whereby every farm labourer was entitled to a certain weekly sum, linked to the price of bread and with due allowance made for his dependants. Theoretically it was an enlightened and logical idea, but the snag lay in the source of the money which was to provide this subsistence income. A proposal to impose a minimum wage was turned down, and instead it was decided to place the onus on the parish rates. Within a few decades almost every labourer in the parish was a pauper on parish relief. *The Village Labourer* (J.L. and Barbara Hammond) gives an instance of how it worked out in 1816, as illustrated by a report to the Board of Agriculture. One observer reported that in his district, "the overseer called a meeting every Saturday, when he put up each labourer by name to auction, and they were let generally at from 1s 6d to 2s per week and their provisions, their families being supported by the parish".

By this time the Napoleonic Wars were over, and corn prices began to fall catastrophically. While the estate-owners, letting out their land at wartime rents, continued to prosper, many of the farmers were at their wits' end to meet all their commitments in the matter of rents, tithes, taxes and rates. Bankruptcies were common, land began to fall into dereliction, and to the other woes of the now landless labourers was added unemployment. The desire to encourage these half-paupers to emigrate is thus explained.

In an effort to stabilize the situation, the Government passed a series of Corn Laws, the first in 1815, to maintain the price of corn. Naturally they caused much misery and resentment in the towns as well as among the rural poor, and an antagonism which was beginning between the urban and rural populations was deepened and fostered. From this time onward, the countryman, as typified by the farmer, could except little sympathy from the urban voter, except in time of war, and even now an innate antagonism still exists in some quarters.

Through all the turbulence and turmoil, a leaven of new ideas produced a fundamental revolution in agriculture, the basic industry of the countryside. The mechanical inventions of the industrial towns were paralleled by the invention of new machines in the service of farming. Jethro Tull, early in the eighteenth century, developed a seed-drill and a horse-drawn hoe. Robert Ransome in 1785 patented a process for producing tempered cast-iron ploughshares. The Reverend Patrick Bell, of Carmylie, Forfarshire, invented a prototype reaper for harvesting corn in 1826. Andrew Meikle, of East Lothian, is usually credited with the invention of the mechanical threshing-machine, in 1786, though other researchers were working on the same principles a decade or two earlier. Steam power was introduced to the farm, first to drive mills and then for other purposes, in the 1760s.

Few if any of these machines and the more elaborate ones which followed could have found a place on the fragmented farms of the pre-enclosure days.

A similar revolution took place in the breeding of livestock. In the middle years of the eighteenth century a Leicestershire farmer, Robert Bakewell, worked out the principles of controlled breeding by selection. He decided in advance what characteristics he intended to breed for, picked the likeliest parent stock and then ruthlessly culled any progeny which did not conform. Inbreeding was permissible so long as it resulted in the right type. And the programme was consistently followed for generation after generation. Bakewell did not work in a vacuum. Other Midland stock breeders were pursuing the same idea, and by the end of the century the principles were widely accepted and followed.

A dramatic improvement in the quality of farm livestock naturally followed. Specific breeds were established and kept pure by the meticulous keeping of pedigree records. Bakewell worked primarily with Longhorn cattle and Leicester sheep. Soon other breeders were working on the Shorthorn, the Hereford, the Devon, the Ayrshire, the Jersey and other breeds of cattle, while scores of breeds of sheep were being evolved. Pigs and poultry, too, attracted 'improvers', and horse-breeders brought their skill to bear in perfecting the huge Shires, Suffolks and Clydesdales.

Mistakes were made, naturally. Bakewell himself sacrificed valuable other characteristics in developing the Longhorn as a beef breed. Some of the early Shorthorn breeders put too great a store on sheer obesity, which for a time developed into a grotesque fashion. The 'improvers' of the primitive Wiltshire Horn sheep did their job so well that their new version of the breed, superior though it was in most respects, no longer had the hardihood to exist on the poor chalk downs which had been its traditional habitat; and in consequence the breed came near to extinction.

In general, though, the pioneer work of the breeders was a notable achievement. The principles that guided them have been the basis of animal breeding throughout the world ever since. Their achievements would hardly have been possible under the old dispensation, which predicated that all the livestock of a parish should run together for much of the year.

The application of similar principles to the breeding of farm crops came at a somewhat later date, and with certain plants, notably grasses, has had to wait till the present century. However, as early at 1820 a Suffolk farm labourer, John Andrews, of Debenham, took the inspired step of retaining a particularly fine ear of barley he happened to notice and of growing a generation or two from it in succeeding years. The experiment was seen by a Dr Charles Chevalier, who took it over and developed a fine new variety of barley, which he named after himself, Chevalier.

Of greater importance than the development of new varieties of crops, however, was the adoption of the principles of crop rotation. The old three-course rotation of the open-field system, namely, wheat, barley and fallow, was superseded first by a four-course rotation and then by a whole range of experimental ones, which, indeed, are still continuing. We have already noted the introduction of sainfoin in the middle of the seventeenth century. About the same time, a Surrey landowner, Sir Richard Weston, was doing his best to popularize red clover and turnips as field crops. His work was taken up in the early eighteenth-century by Lord Townshend, of Norfolk, who introduced the Norfolk four-course rotation, which ran: wheat; roots; barley; seeds.

The seeds were the seeds of grasses and clovers, now elevated, perhaps for the first time, to the status of a widely-cultivated field crop. The roots were turnips. By employing the new rotation, Coke of Holkham (later Earl of Leicester) transformed poor rye-growing land of north-western Norfolk into highly fertile wheat-growing soil, and incidentally ably publicized the system.

The advantages of the new system, and of the others developed from it, were twofold. In the first place, they helped the soil to renew its fertility between each grain crop. Secondly, they provided additional crops for feeding livestock. The importance of this second factor is that it enabled far greater numbers of animals than before to be kept, and indeed fattened, during the winter. No longer was the holocaust of surplus cattle and sheep at Martinmas necessary.

Turnips were instrumental in greatly extending the area of land under cultivation. Soils formerly thought too poor for cropping were now brought under the plough. For turnips, grown in rows as a field crop and thinned by hoeing, could be eaten in the fields by sheep confined by hurdle pens. The pens or folds were moved daily, each supplying a day's ration for the flock. By this means every square yard of the field was trodden and manured by the sheep, which thus acquired the title 'the golden hoof'. In the second half of the eighteenth century, swedes, which are hardier than turnips, were introduced, so extending the grazing season throughout the winter, though swedes could also be stored in clamps for use in severe weather.

Other crops experimented with in the innovating eighteenth century included cabbages, mangolds, kohl rabi and rape. The last mentioned was increasingly grown for its oil, which, together with the oil from linseed, was processed into oilcake. This concentrated food not only fattened cattle with wonderful efficiency but also had a by-product in rich manure. A rye-grass and red clover mixture, sometimes with the addition of cocksfoot grass, from an annual sowing produced a heavy hay-crop, which formed the basis of roughage for the winter ration. In the fattening yards of lowland Britain, cattle fattened in winter even better than on summer grazing.

At the root of all these impressive improvements lay the fact that farmers were now producing for profit, not subsistence. Their crops and livestock were produced primarily for market, and not necessarily a market on the doorstep, at the nearest market town. For the urban populations of London and the big manufacturing towns were now entirely divorced from country life. They had no hope of feeding themselves but were entirely dependent on what was brought in from outside.

That the new race of commercial farmers made a good job of feeding them is demonstrated by the rapid growth of population already mentioned. On the whole, the fields of Britain produced enough food for both rural and urban populations, even though the distribution was often faulty. Whether it could have been done under the old open-field system is at least very doubtful. The detested enclosures were probably a necessary evil before Britain could become a great industrial nation.

The new system involved the transport of large quantities of food from country to town, which called for better roads. By ancient custom each parish had maintained its own roads, after a fashion. An enactment of the sixteenth century, which was not repealed till 1835, required every landholder in a parish to contribute four days' work per year to road repairs, but in most places it tended to be a dead letter. In the seventeenth century a new system was devised to replace it. The first Turnpike Act was passed in 1663, and from about the middle of the eighteenth century Turnpike Acts followed each other as quickly as Enclosure Acts. The principle was that in return for constructing and maintaining a good road, a 'turnpike trust' could erect toll-gates at either end and charge tolls for the use of the road, the money in theory being used for improving the highway.

Turnpike trusts became a highly capitalistic affair. They were usually formed by local gentry, who put up the necessary capital in shares. Once the road was ready and the barriers installed, the rights of toll collection were put up for auction. There were individuals who made a business of investing in turnpike tolls, one celebrated Manchester gentleman doing so to the reputed tune of £50,000 a year – an enormous sum in those days. He would install a toll-collector in each lodge, at a wage of around twenty to twenty-five shillings a week (quite good pay for that period), and employed a troop of collectors to collect the tolls from them. Legal quarrels were commonplace, and it was said that at least half the money taken in tolls went into the pockets of lawyers, surveyors and clerks. What with this drain on the exchequer and the payment of the collectors, either the initial investors went short or the road maintenance suffered. Human nature suggests the latter.

The situation became highly complex. A writer in the late nineteenth century, recalling the turnpikes in the days of his youth, said that the town of Aylesbury, which he knew well, was so ringed with turnpikes that it was impossible to take a horse outside the town for exercise without paying a toll. These turnpikes belonged to no fewer than seven independent trusts, each of which maintained its expensive set of officials. In 1840 England had 22,000 miles of turnpike roads, with nearly eight thousand toll gates – which meant a toll-gate at every $2\frac{3}{4}$ miles.

The whole cumbersome apparatus was eventually swept aside by the coming of the railways. While it lasted, however, it did effect an improvement in the standard of road-building and provided a background against which Macadam and other pioneers could work out their revolutionary methods. Macadam was Surveyor to the British Turnpike Trust in 1816. Numerous toll-houses still survive as a reminder of the Turnpike Age, and in places one may find a notice marking the demarcation line between a turnpike road and some other, usually a bridge erected by another authority.

In the first half of the nineteenth century the usual turnpike tolls were at about the following levels: $1\frac{1}{2}$ pence for a horse; $4\frac{1}{2}$ pence for a vehicle drawn by one horse; 9 pence for a two-horse vehicle; and so on. The charges bore particularly severely on farmers, who frequently took a four-horse wagon to market. The payment of the toll entitled the vehicle to use the turnpike road till midnight, after which the driver paid again, but in many instances if a farmer returned from market with a load different from that which he took in, as would be only natural, he was charged a second toll. And sometimes he would have to pass two or more turnpike gates on the way to town.

Naturally every user of the highway was interested in ways and means of bypassing toll-gates. In highly cultivated districts the feat was difficult, and the turnpike-owners had a vested interest in blocking the gaps, but long-distance traffic travelled where possible on unfenced tracks over the uncultivated uplands.

While grain had of necessity to be carted in waggons, livestock travelled on their own feet. An important and familiar feature of the eighteenth- and early nineteenth-century countryside were immense droves of animals on their way to market. One of the main drovers' routes was from Wales to London and the fairs and markets in the vicinity of the capital. It is estimated that in the eighteenth century thirty thousand cattle passed through Herefordshire on their way south-eastwards every autumn. Sheep were even more numerous, a single flock often comprising fifteen hundred to two thousand animals. Even pigs were driven long distances across country. Enormous numbers are said to have walked to Bristol market from Wales, there to be purchased by fatteners in Somerset and Dorset who then sent them on another long journey to London. A check on the numbers of pigs passing along a turnpike road at Beckhampton, Wiltshire, *en route* for London, in 1830 put the total at 14,500. At the end of the eighteenth century at least 100,000 cattle and probably some 150,000 sheep crossed the border from Scotland into England annually. Some of the cattle were of Irish origin, over ten thousand a year being landed at two ports in Wigtownshire alone.

Nor were cattle, sheep and pigs the only livestock on the move in eighteenth-century Britain. Very large numbers of turkeys and geese walked to market on their own two feet. Daniel Defoe, writing early in the eighteenth century, testifies to counting three hundred droves of turkeys passing in one season over Stratford Bridge. "These droves, as they say, generally contain from three hundred to a thousand each drove, so that one may suppose them to contain five hundred, one with another, which is 150,000 in all." The Stratford Bridge mentioned is the one over the River Lea, on the north-eastern approaches to London. The flocks of geese were equally large. Defoe asserts,

> A prodigious number are brought up to London in droves from the furthest parts of Norfolk, even from the fenn-country about Lynn, Downham, Wisbech and the Washes; as also from all the east side of Norfolk and Suffolk, of whom 'tis very frequent now to meet droves, with a thousand, sometimes two thousand, in a drove. They begin to drive them generally in August, by which time the harvest is almost over, and the geese may feed on the stubbles as they go. Thus they hold on to the end of October, when the roads begin to be too stiff and deep for their broad feet and short legs to march in.

Some of the Fenland geese, however, were diverted to the opposite direction, to Nottingham Goose Fair, which, held at Michaelmas, lasted for twenty-one days and in its heyday attracted at least twenty thousand geese. Other big flocks of geese travelled up to London from the West Country, for at Ilchester, Somerset, "a saddler and harness-maker made boots of soft leather for the travelling geese. These boots were carried by the drovers and placed on the feet of geese that became lame or suffered damage to their feet in the long walks".

Cattle and sheep seem to have averaged about fifteen miles a day in flat country; pigs six to ten miles. In hilly country ten to twelve miles a day was perhaps more general. Sheep flocks on the road down from Scotland were supposed to rest twice a day and to have a full day's rest every third day. The flocks and herds were not hurried, but a reasonably steady rate of progress had to be maintained. The drovers followed well-recognized routes and had standing arrangements with farmers willing to allow their animals to rest overnight. 'Halfpenny' as a field name is usually an indication that here the charge for pasturing cattle overnight was a halfpenny a beast. Rivers were crossed by swimming or fording, or, in the case of a wide and deep river, on rafts. Pigs were sometimes "fed with horse-beans in the street". Catering for turkeys at night imposed a slight problem, for the birds would insist on going to roost in trees.

Drovers were licensed and had to be mature men ("over thirty years old") of good character and temperament, for they frequently had charge of animals valued at thousands of pounds. On their long journeys they undertook commissions in both directions, carrying news as well as commodities and being often joined by other travellers. On their return journeys they would frequently take back breeding sheep and cattle, such as choice rams for crossing, for farmers *en route*, and northern drovers did a considerable trade in donkeys. The droving traffic was highly organized and was catered for by series of inns and alehouses along the drovers' routes.

The peak period of the drovers was around the middle of the eighteenth century. By the end of the century, although perhaps the volume of traffic had increased, the drovers were finding their traffic impeded and frustrated by the rapidly growing number of enclosures and turnpike tolls. Their epoch came to an end with the coming of the railways in the 1840s, though flocks of sheep made the journey from Wales to Harrow, Middlesex, until the end of the nineteenth century.

Several further examples of land improvement and reclamation under the stimulus of farming for profit remain to be noticed. Probably the most important was the reclamation of the Fens. Although this largely antedated the great period of enclosures by a century or so, it was due to the same concept of capitalist farming. The expense of draining and reclamation was so enormous that only a large-scale and heavily financed scheme had any hope of success.

The Fens were vast morasses, occupying parts of six counties and created by rivers unable to escape to the sea. The great rivers of the Midlands meandered all over the lowlying plain (which was approximately seventy-six miles on its north-south axis, thirty miles on its east-west one), silting up their channels, creating new ones, breaking out in floods and then abandoning the lakes they had formed. It was an amphibious region of every phase of swamp and fen, with here and there fertile islands rising out of the watery wilderness. None could approach these islands on foot across the treacherous quagmires, and none but the marshmen could follow the devious and constantly changing waterways. On them grew up flourishing communities of farmers, fishermen and fowlers, sheltering under the great Fenland abbeys, as at Thorney and Crowland. Ely's magnificent cathedral dominates the southern fens.

The obvious task was to take the water away to the sea by the most direct means possible, which meant digging straight channels through the marshlands to The Wash. Charles I called over Dutch experts, headed by Cornelius Vermuyden, and encouraged the Earl of Bedford to set up a joint-stock company to finance such a project. The scheme aroused fierce hostility from the marshmen, who saw their way of life threatened. Riots occurred, and dykes and earthworks were destroyed by night. Then the Civil War intervened, and the scheme was temporarily shelved.

Afterwards, however, it was quickly resurrected, and by 1653 the Bedford Rivers had been cut. They are a good example of the Fenland drainage system. They run parallel, about half a mile apart, for a course of about twenty miles from Earith, in Huntingdonshire, to Denver, Norfolk, and supply a short cut across a great bend of the River Ouse. Between the two lies a long narrow strip of rough grazing, technically known as a 'wash'. This acts as a kind of safety-valve. When the levels of water in the two rivers, flowing above the surrounding countryside, become menacingly high, the pressure on the banks is relieved by diverting water into the wash. Until the wash itself is completely flooded, there is no danger to the neighbouring country.

With the fertile drained land lying lower than the level of the river beds, water from every little drain has to be pumped up into the larger drains by countless pumping stations and finally, by a giant pumping plant, into the sea. This problem increased with the shrinkage of the black fen soil, due to the drying-out of the peat. The windmills constructed to do the pumping in the eighteenth century formed a picturesque feature of the landscape, but they have now nearly all been replaced.

The success of the Bedford scheme, which was completed in its original form before 1660, inspired other similar projects, notably in the northern Fens. The reclaimed land proved to be some of the best in all England, capable of producing not only good wheat crops but also heavy yields of potatoes, carrots and other vegetables for the markets of London and the Midlands. So a new industry developed. More and more Fenland was drained and cultivated until now the only section of the original amphibious countryside left as it used to be is the 320 acres of Wicken Fen, now National Trust property and a haven for wild life.

An interesting but minor contribution to land reclamation was provided by the winning of land from the sea. Silt brought down by the rivers tends to form mud-flats around their mouths, and these have, from the eighteenth century onwards, been fenced in by earthworks and brought under cultivation when sufficient soil has accumulated. A traditional method of claiming land from the sea was 'warping', as practised by the Humber estuary, where masses of silt brought down by the swift-flowing Yorkshire rivers is shifted about by tide and currents. A bank of earth is erected around the area of mud-flat to be reclaimed, but with a narrow opening through which the tide can be admitted at will. Each tide deposits a layer of silt a few millimetres thick. It is estimated that, by using all practicable tides, a stratum of 'warp', as the silt is called, fourteen inches thick, will be accumulated in about eighteen months. The soil thus trapped is exceptionally fertile and seldom requires fortifying by manure for at least a generation.

A somewhat similar idea was from the early seventeenth century onwards widely employed in obtaining maximum production of grass in river valleys. The meadows thus treated were known as 'floating' or 'water' meadows, and their annual flooding was called 'drowning'. It could be practised at any time of the year but was normally reserved for winter, for the purpose of producing an early crop of grass for grazing sheep.

In a typical narrow valley, such as are common in the chalk country, the whole width of the valley from the foot of the escarpment on one side to the foot of the escarpment on the other would be levelled off and transformed into flat meadows. Down the centre of the valley wriggled the main stream, and side channels skirted the edge of the meadows on either side. Between these main channels the meadows were cut up into a network of parallel ditches, four or five yards apart and at two levels. The 'carriages' ran along the top of a slight bank, their surface about level with the water-level in the main streams.

The 'drains', running parallel to the carriages, were three or four feet below their level. When the hatches were manipulated to let the water from the main river into the meadows, the carriages were soon brimful, their water spilling over their lips, trickling down the banks and finding its way into the drains, which carried it back eventually to the main channel. The entire surface of the meadow was thus covered with a slowly-moving blanket of water, which effectively prevented its ever freezing in a normal English winter. In consequence, in a meadow flooded in December, the grass kept growing all through the winter, providing an oasis of green in a sere and sombre world. About mid-March the hatches would be closed, leaving a rich pasturage for sheep a good month or so before any grass was available in upland fields.

Water-meadows were being laid out on manorial domains before the general spate of enclosures. Their introduction is attributed by some early agricultural writers to 'Dutchmen', which seems likely enough. The system seems to have been developed in Herefordshire and to have been well known there by the middle of the seventeenth century. In the heart of the chalk country, in Wiltshire, Thomas Davis of Longleat, writing in 1811, gives most of the credit to a Squire Baverstock who lived in the Wylye valley in the early years of the eighteenth century. Davis says,

> An imperfect scheme of watering had undoubtedly been practised before that period, ... but the regular mode in which those systems are now conducted are certainly not very ancient. Many old farmers, who have died within the memory of man, remembered when neither the water-meadow nor the sheep-fold was managed on any regular plan.

After the early grazing, the water-meadows could be relied on to give a good hay-crop. In a later age, however, they had the disadvantage of making the use of mechanized grass-cutting equipment almost impossible, so when most of them fell into dereliction during the great agricultural depression of the 1920s and early 1930s, they were never thereafter restored. However, a few have survived and are interesting examples of high farming at its most efficient, as well as being havens for all manner of bird life in a hard winter.

One other aspect of the age of improvement remains to be noticed. From about the middle of the eighteenth century onwards, the movement to construct navigational canals gathered increasing momentum. Within about eight years from that date over four thousand miles were added to England's inland waterways.

The idea of canals was, of course, not new. The Romans had introduced them, and in the seventeenth century the stupendous scheme for draining the Fens was planned around drainage canals which could also be used for navigation. Canals constructed primarily to take water-borne traffic were of two sorts, namely short reaches designed to bypass some obstacle, such as a weir or broken water, and cross-country waterways.

One of the earliest canals of the industrial age was of the latter sort. It was financed by the Duke of Bridgewater to carry coal from his mines at Worsley to Manchester, just over ten miles away. It was designed by a canal-building genius, James Brindley, who solved the problems of making an impervious canal-bed and of carrying a canal over a water barrier by an aqueduct. Opened in 1761, it was known as the Bridgewater Canal and attracted much attention, especially as it made the Duke a great deal of money.

Soon other landowners were similarly engaged, and by 1835, when the last major canal (the Birmingham and Liverpool Junction) was opened, Britain was criss-crossed by a network of canals which made it possible to travel from the Irish Sea and the Bristol Channel across to the North Sea by several alternative routes. A new feature of the rural scene in those days was the teams of 'navigators' (from which term we get the word 'navvies'), itinerant workers, frequently Irish, who dug the canals. Although their work has now been mellowed by time and become a treasured part of the rural heritage, at the time it constituted a major upheaval, obliterating rural landmarks, altering field boundaries and in some instances, reshaping the face of the countryside past recognition.

Canal traffic was inexpensive but slow. At first the barges were pulled along by men, who sometimes had to 'leg' them through tunnels, by lying on their backs and pushing on the roof of the tunnel with their feet. From about 1800 horses were the chief motive-power, usually slow old horses well past their prime. From the point of view of efficiency, the English canals had one drawback, their narrowness. Brindley, the pioneer, chose to make his first canal 7½ feet wide, and his example was almost universally followed. This had the effect of limiting to about thirty tons the load which a 'narrow-boat' could carry.

Canals were made to carry bulky and heavy loads at a leisurely pace, and for a time they were supreme in that sphere. They had little competition until the coming of the railways, which, however, quickly altered the picture. In the rough, tough early Victorian era, the new railway barons were not content with honest competition. They frequently used their wealth to buy up stock in the canal companies, in order to close them down or, more subtly, to raise their tolls to prohibitive levels. So the canals, after a brief spell of glory, were eased out of the commercial life of the nation and became quiet backwaters, to experience a new lease of life more than a hundred years later, as recreational amenities.

7

The Victorian Countryside

The years following the Battle of Waterloo saw the rural landowners at the zenith of their power. A continued spate of enclosure acts was rapidly transforming what was left of the old pattern of rural Britain into the familiar countryside of today. The former peasants, now reduced to the status of labourers, though by no means docile and inarticulate, were being kept firmly in their place. Man-traps and spring-guns protected the landowner's game on what was formerly common land. For carrying nets at night to snare a rabbit or hare, a man could be sentenced to seven years' transportation. For sheep-stealing he was, of course, hanged. In 1830 the much-abused and desperate labourers rose in a spontaneous revolt, the immediate cause of which was the introduction of threshing-machines, which they concluded would greatly reduce the amount of winter work available to them and so make them even more dependent on parish relief. Mobs went around the countryside smashing the hated machines and demanding better wages and other concessions. The rising was ruthlessly suppressed. In the trials which followed, reminiscent of the circuit of Judge Jeffreys, nine men were condemned to be hanged and between 450 and 600 transported to Australia. Parliament, its membership composed exclusively of one class, supported the severest measures. The fetters of the rural labourer were fastened even more securely. And when, six years later, a handful of irrepressible trouble-makers had the temerity actually to form an embryo trade union in the little Dorset village of Tolpuddle, the authorities stamped on it as they would have done on a tarantula.

But nemesis was about to descend on the rural autocrats.

They had driven enormous numbers of former peasants into the new manufacturing towns. Out of sight, out of mind. However, there they were, alive and requiring to be fed. When, after Waterloo, the price of corn fell dramatically, Parliament quickly passed a Corn Law to force it to artificially high levels. It then discovered that it had sown dragon's teeth. The urban population, from the labouring poor (who had no power) to the bankers, merchants and new capitalists (who had), was bitterly and violently opposed to any measures against cheap food. As members of Parliament went to the House of Commons to vote for the Bill, they were set upon and beaten up by mobs who had been egged on by speeches by industrialists and bankers.

For the next thirty years battle royal was waged between the rural and urban interests, culminating in 1846 in the repeal of the Corn Laws. Meantime another conflict had flared up, between the same two parties, on the very composition of the legislature. The franchise was based on ancient custom rather than on modern actualities. Tiny country towns returned one or two members of Parliament, with the classic example of Old Sarum, the abandoned mediaeval hill-top earthwork near Salisbury, having two representatives although it had not a single inhabitant, while populous new towns such as Sheffield and Manchester were without representation. The Reform Bills, abolishing 'rotten boroughs' and establishing a more equitable franchise, were opposed tooth and nail by the old rural aristocracy, led by the Duke of Wellington, who rightly saw their privileges threatened. But, by expelling the old peasant population to the towns, they now found that they had driven them beyond reach. The labourers on their estates they could keep in proper subjection, but they could not do the same to the workers in the factories of Lancashire, the mills of Yorkshire and the mines of Northumberland. In 1832, after a winter of violent unrest throughout the country, the Reform Act was passed and the absolute power of the country landowner was drastically curbed if not finally broken.

These political conflicts of a past age had more to do with the subsequent shape of the countryside than is superficially apparent. Before the enclosures, under the old order, there had been some coherence and unity between the various interests of the nation. When the population was fairly evenly dispersed around the country in small towns and villages, there was at least some mutual understanding of problems. But now an urban population had grown up which was entirely divorced from rural affairs. It had no knowledge of the traditional way of life in the countryside and was interested only in the cheap food of which the fields beyond the smoking chimneys of the town were the source. The nation was divided into two opposed sections, very unequal in strength under any democratic system which depended ultimately on the counting of heads. Now, in the first trial of strength, the towns had demonstrated their new power. By depopulating the countryside, the landowners had ensured that they would therefore forever be in a minority.

For three decades after the passing of the Reform Act, the countryside remained relatively peaceful and prosperous. Poverty was still the lot of the farm labourer, but he had shot his bolt in 1830 and 1836 and had relapsed into a kind of fatalistic quiescence. Meantime farming flourished. This was afterwards regarded as the Golden Age of high farming. The reason was that, with reforms gradually improving the lot of the factory workers, the urban population was continuing to increase prodigiously. At the same time their purchasing power was also increasing. The food to feed them could only come from Britain's farms. There was nowhere else in Europe with a sufficient surplus. So all the innovations and improvements in farming technique and practice, the better livestock, the bigger crops, the more efficient rotations, were needed to keep pace with the ever-growing demand. Cultivation was extended until even the steep hillsides were ploughed and sown to grain. The countryside had its fair share in that progress which the Victorians came to regard as inevitable.

A thoughtful observer might well have asked himself, where will it all end? He would have read gloomily the pessimistic predictions of Thomas Malthus and would have felt that their accuracy was being demonstrated before his very eyes. For the population of England and Wales had increased from 8,893,000 in 1801 to 17,928,000 in 1851. Moreover, more than half of them were living in towns and producing no food at all. Even with the most efficient farming methods, there must be a limit to the number of mouths which the fields of Britain could feed, and that limit would soon be reached.

Then, just as disaster appeared to be imminent, salvation came from a quarter which had not been considered. The alternative destination for dispossessed peasants in the eighteenth and nineteenth centuries was the new lands overseas. In an ever-increasing stream, they poured across the oceans to people America, Canada, Australia, New Zealand and South Africa. In countries which offered reasonable rewards for their natural energy, thrift and ingenuity, they carved farms out of the wilderness, reared large families under pioneer conditions and soon began to produce a surplus of food. In 1875 the first shiploads of wheat from the prairies arrived in Britain. Within the next ten years it had become an avalanche, and the development of refrigerated ships had made possible the importation of meat as well. The revenge of the peasant was complete.

Prices toppled. Between 1875 and 1896 those of all cereals were approximately halved. The catastrophe coincided with a series of dull, wet summers and consequent bad harvests. Agriculture entered a depression from which, for ever afterwards, it was only to emerge in time of war, when supplies of food from overseas were in danger of being completely cut off. Within those first twenty years the corn acreage dropped by some twenty-five per cent, rents by at least twenty per cent, and more than twenty-five per cent of employed workers had to find other jobs. Royal Commissions were set up to study the situation but could achieve nothing. Britain's booming manufacturing industries maintained their competitiveness by keeping costs low, and cheap food was an essential consideration. About the source of the food the consumers cared nothing. They had as little sympathy with and understanding of the problems of the countryside as the country landowners had shown to their ancestors when the enclosures were in progress.

Some slight alleviation occurred around the turn of the century, partly owing to the pressures of the Boer War and partly to increasing urban prosperity, so the Britain which entered the First World War was not too badly equipped agriculturally to cope with the new, clamorous demands for food. Under the threat of the U-boat, a rapid revival of farming occurred. The wheat acreage increased by a million during the war years, the oat acreage by 1,100,000, and all farm livestock (except pigs, which lived to a great extent on imported feeding-stuffs) multiplied. As the war drew to an end in 1918, the Government passed a Corn Production Act which had the same purpose as the Corn Laws after the Napoleonic Wars, to protect home agriculture from a sudden slump in the prices of commodities.

The Act met with the same fate. Under pressure from the urban electorate, it was jettisoned only three years later, in 1921. Thereafter the countryside went into rapid decline. Fields were hardly worth cultivating; livestock was hardly worth keeping; great areas of Britain fell into complete dereliction. In farmers' meetings, speakers advanced plausible arguments to prove that land was worth nothing; it was just space out-of-doors. Early in the 1930s a distraint order for non-payment of tithe was served on a farmer and landowner near Basingstoke, Hampshire. On his entire estate of over nine hundred acres, the bailiffs could find nothing at all to seize, neither crops nor cattle nor agricultural implements nor even gates or fences. Nothing. Britain was reverting to grassland, scrub and forest.

We arrive now at a time when a contribution can be made by living memory, including that of the present author. Having been born in 1914, just before the First World War, my earliest memories are of a poverty-stricken village that formed an oasis in a sea of dereliction. A photograph of the village taken in the early 1880s, before the depression had had time to bite, shows a well-kept, prosperous-looking place, its pastures grazed and its hedges neatly laid and trimmed, far different from the shaggy, untidy village of my boyhood.

Most readers will feel an affinity with some corner of rural Britain, a farm, village or hamlet which ancestors a few generations back called home. In perusing the following account of my native village in the 1920s and 1930s and in the memories my father had of it in the late nineteenth century, may I invite them to translate it into terms of the place they know best. Almost every detail could be duplicated a thousand times in similar parishes throughout the kingdom.

This village in which I was born and reared and which I therefore know best is Pitton, near Salisbury, Wiltshire. It is a chalkland village, lying in the last little valley of Salisbury Plain near its frontier with the clays of the New Forest. In a great arc from east through south to west lie extensive woodlands, the survivals of ancient forests. On the other arc, from east through north to west, extended the rolling downlands, like a petrified ocean swell for what seemed to a boy an interminable distance beyond the horizon.

Almost every phase in the history of the countryside is represented in this microcosm of it. The village green, long since encroached upon, was a section of an ancient green trackway leading, according to local tradition, to a port on Southampton Water. Here, on a day nearly four thousand years ago, a man died, probably a violent death, and was buried. His grave was discovered in the 1950s. Perhaps he was on his way to or from Stonehenge, which, less than ten miles away, was either brand new or still under construction.

Three miles to the north-west, on a hill crest, is the Early Iron Age hill-fort of Figsbury. Enclosing fifteen acres, this earthwork may originally have been a kind of cattle corral, its ramparts later strengthened, for excavations have revealed no evidence of permanent habitation. At about the same distance to the north-east are prehistoric flint-mines on Easton Down, and an associated settlement of people who lived in timber houses over sunken foundations, who grew corn and kept as domestic animals cattle, sheep, pigs and dogs. A mound only a mile or so from Pitton has proved on excavation to be a long barrow, and other round barrows dotted around the vicinity have yet to be investigated.

The Romans constructed a major road from Winchester to Sorbiodunum and the west. It can still be clearly traced for almost its entire length, and sections of it are in use as modern roads. On a hill overlooking the Pitton section, a Romano-British village flourished in the third and fourth centuries AD, possibly earlier as well. It was inhabited by poor, independent peasant folk, the outlines of whose little rectangular fields are still visible on the hillsides all around. The village cemetery was excavated a few years ago and proved to be an arc of graves around a deep pit which presumably was considered an entrance to the underworld. Some of the graves were inhumations, some cremations, the ashes being deposited in urns. Some of the corpses had apparently suffered injury or had been killed by decapitation. Some had coins in their mouths, to pay the ferryman. One old woman had bones twisted and deformed by arthritis and may well have been considered a witch. The men were buried in board coffins, with their boots on, but evidently poverty compelled them to economize on the coffins, for the minimum of six iron nails was used for each. The downs in the vicinity are criss-crossed by sunken tracks which are probably of the same period, but the village site itself has not been excavated.

On the other side of Pitton, on the wooded slopes leading southwards towards the New Forest, once stood a group of Roman villas, the sites of three of which have been found and partially excavated, while it is thought that more existed. The land here was heavy, fertile and well-watered, in strong contrast with the meagre, thin soils of the chalk downland by the Roman road. When the villas fell into ruin and the land into dereliction at the end of the Roman era, a dense growth first of scrub and then of forest trees sprang up to obliterate all traces of the former country estates. As none of the coins found in the hill-top cemetery was dated later than about AD 360, it is presumed that the Romano-British village also was abandoned soon after that date, perhaps as a result of the great irruption of the Picts, Scots and Saxons in 367. But the population was probably not exterminated, for there seems to have been a continuity of occupation at Winterslow, two or three miles to the east and straddling the Roman road. This is one of the few hill-top villages that bridged the gap into Saxon Wessex.

The Saxons advanced up the rivers and formed their settlements in the river valleys. In this district they came up the Avon and formed very early settlements at Britford and Longford, Britford being mentioned in documents as early as AD 670. They also probed up the little River Bourne, which is a tributary of the Avon, founding a string of villages along its banks.

In the course of time these riverside farms and villages expanded uphill in long, narrow strip fields on either side of the stream, as described in an earlier chapter (see page 55). In the direction of Pitton, the Winterbourne farms reached over a subsidiary valley and to the hill-crest less than a mile off the other village. The eventual boundary seems deliberately to have taken in the site of the old Romano-British village. Meantime from Alderbury, on the hither side of the Avon from Longford and Britford, settlers moved out northwards to form settlements at West and East Grimstead and eventually at Farley, 'the far meadow'. They were working away from the river along the southern edge of a dense forest, later known as the Royal Forest of Clarendon. Beyond Farley, and on the other side of a long hill, lies Pitton, but local opinion is that this place was settled from the old hill village of Winterslow. As late as the end of the nineteenth century, a tradition of antipathy between Pitton and Farley persisted (although by this time they had been combined to form one parish), and local people would testify, "We marries with Winterslow but not with they down at Farley." (It must be admitted, though, that the parish registers do not entirely bear out their contention.)

Early churches were often built on sites sacred to the old pagan religion, and I have speculated on that having happened at Pitton. The churchyard enclosure is still semi-circular and may once have been a complete ring. It was situated on the bank of a pond which once was fed by probably the only permanent spring in the valley. One can imagine the villagers from the Romano-British site on the hill plodding down to the sacred spring in the valley on holy days and worshipping there. Later the religious traditions were strong enough to send a new generation of settlers down from Winterslow to form a settlement around the old shrine. It might have happened, but it is all conjecture. Probably we shall never know.

At any rate, all the villages were in existence early in the ninth century, before the time of Alfred the Great. The Danes were here soon afterwards, as we know from the name Dunley, 'Dane ley', given to a lane near the village. That could, however, be anticipated, for the raiders must often have travelled along the Roman road.

We do not have a Domesday Book record, for the following reason: Pitton, Farley, Alderbury and the adjoining villages were forest villages, satellites of the Forest of Clarendon, which was evidently a royal chase from an early date, perhaps from the time of the Saxon kings. The name Pitton is derived from 'Putta-ton', the settlement of Putta, which was a personal name. However, 'Putta' also means 'a hawk'. It is quite in keeping with early practice that a man should be nicknamed 'Putta', 'a hawk', but, on the other hand, this may have been the place where the royal hawks were kept.

The orientation of Pitton, Farley and the Grimsteads was always towards the Forest. Even in late Victorian and Edwardian times, much of the population derived its living from the woods, either by direct employment or more commonly as independent craftsmen cutting underwood for hurdles and other purposes. The barbed tips of hunting arrows of mediaeval date have been found in village gardens.

The Norman kings, perhaps beginning with William the Conqueror, built a hunting-lodge on a hill, still known as King Manor, on the far side of the Forest from Pitton. It was a singular building in those troublous times, being almost completely unfortified. Apart from one tower, it seems to have been a range of single-storeyed edifices rambling over, eventually, about eighteen acres. Its history is remarkably well documented for the reason that it was inhabited only intermittently. The King and his Court evidently came there for hunting when the realm was quiet. Sometimes the visits were fairly frequent; at other times long periods elapsed without a royal appearance, and the palace fell into semi-dereliction. Then the king would send down a commission to report on the state of disrepair, and plans would be drawn up for renovations. Many of these documents survive, and in the 1930s archaeologists from the Department of Mediaeval Art at London University spent a series of summers excavating the site (then completely buried in forest) and trying to match what they found with the plans they possessed. The outbreak of war in 1939 brought the work to a premature close, but the bulk of it had been completed and was sufficient to give a picture of a mediaeval palace on which a succession of monarchs lavished much love and cash.

At the margin of the woodland, near Alderbury, stood the priory of Ivychurch, occupied by thirteen monks whose duty it was to attend to the spiritual needs of the royal Court in residence at Clarendon Palace. The Black Death killed off twelve of the monks, and the thirteenth duly applied, successfully, to be appointed prior. Another young priest used to walk up from his home at Winterbourne Ford, below Old Sarum, to attend on the king when he was at Clarendon. His name was Thomas à Becket. In later years, after he had been canonized, the path which he trod from Winterbourne to Clarendon was said to be always green.

At intervals during those mediaeval centuries, the Forest as well as the Palace was the subject of surveys. One from the fourteenth and one from the sixteenth century survive. They give the boundaries of the royal chase by detailing the names of lanes, coppices, farms, trees and other landmarks. Most still bear the same names. In most sectors the boundaries of the forest in the 1320s were exactly the same as the boundaries of the Clarendon estate in the 1920s. A formidable deer-leap, constructed along the edge of the woodland where it bordered on arable fields, is still largely extant.

The last king to reside in the Palace was Henry VI, who there suffered a period of insanity. Special quarters had to be built for him, as he was unfit to associate with normal people while the malady lasted. More than a hundred years later, when Elizabeth I went hunting in the Forest, the Palace was too ruinous to be used, even for a picnic. Yet in my youth there were still folk-memories of knights on horseback galloping at night along the old road that linked the Roman road with the Palace. Only by then they had become ghosts.

In the seventeenth century, 1627 to be exact, a boy named Stephen Fox, of peasant or yeoman stock, was born at Farley, Pitton's twin village. Gifted and intelligent, he managed to secure a post in the household of Lord Percy, one of the prominent noblemen of the day, in whose service he took part in the campaigns of the Civil War. He accompanied Charles II into exile, and through all the lean years that the King spent abroad he managed the household finances, achieving miracles with a minimal budget. After the Restoration he was duly rewarded for his loyalty. He became an MP, paymaster-general and a lord commissioner of the treasury and amassed a great fortune. His first family having predeceased him, he married a second time late in life and had twin sons. Of these, one became the first Earl of Ilchester, the other the first Earl of Holland. Farley owes its fine Wren-style church to him, Sir Christopher Wren and Sir Stephen being close friends.

Grown to manhood, the two sons made the villages of their ancestors the nuclei of country estates. The Earl of Ilchester acquired the manors of Pitton and Farley; the Earl of Holland that of Winterslow. The Earl of Ilchester made his country seat on another estate in west Dorset, but the Earl of Holland built a magnificent mansion, surrounded by a park, at Winterslow. It was dogged by misfortune. Twice it was burned down soon after building. After the second disaster, the Earl of Holland abandoned Winterslow and concentrated on another estate nearer London, Holland Park, to the great benefit of his successors. But the Earls of Ilchester retained the lands at Pitton and Farley till 1912.

At some time long before 1819, the fields between Pitton and Farley were enclosed, for an enclosure map of 1819, dealing with the fields on the north side of the parish, refers to them as 'ancient enclosures'. The land was, however, still divided into small strips or blocks of an acre or so apiece, each with its surrounding hedge. The hedges were very broad, some as much as twenty yards, and were valued because of the hazel wood they contained. Hazel in the old rural economy had a wide range of uses, notably for hurdles, thatching spars, pea-sticks, bean-rods and such domestic accessories as clothes'-props. The hedges on the other side of the village, dividing the land enclosed in 1819, are completely different, being narrow lines of hawthorn, protected on one side by a ditch. The character of the hedges of the earlier enclosures suggests a probable date of the sixteenth century, perhaps even earlier.

The parish register begins at about 1650, and the surnames mentioned are those of families still well known in the district. From 1841 onwards, the decennial censuses tabulate their statistics under households, recording the names of the heads of the households and all the children and other dependants living under the same roof. It is thus possible to follow the fortunes of individual families. For instance, in 1841 a sixteen-year-old girl is helping her widowed mother run what was evidently a sort of dame's school in her cottage. Ten years later she has married a farm worker, who in 1841 was recorded as married with two small children. The parish register provides the details of the death of his first wife and the date of his second marriage. The records then overlap with living memory, for villagers alive in the 1920s could remember this second wife as an old lady.

Incidental details, surviving in newspaper reports, legal documents and other sources, help to fill in the picture of village life. In 1816 a lioness escaped from her quarters in a travelling menagerie parked for the night at the Pheasant Inn (then known as The Winterslow Hut), the nearest point to Pitton on the Great West Road. It attacked a stage-coach horse and then took refuge under a granary, from which its intrepid attendants extracted it, tying its legs and pulling it out on a sack. A passenger on the coach went insane with fear and had to be sent to an asylum. A Newfoundland dog who attacked the lioness was regarded as the hero of the event. And the unfortunate horse with its open wounds was exhibited in Salisbury. The episode attracted a great deal of publicity, and a number of paintings of it still survive. The villagers of Pitton and Winterslow used regularly to walk the two miles or so to Winterslow Hut to down a pint, meet the stage-coach and heard the latest news from London.

A legal battle around the turn of the nineteenth and twentieth centuries concerned the rights of the villagers of Pitton and Farley to use footpaths through Clarendon Woods. The then owner of the estate tried to exclude them altogether, but the villagers assembled all the oldest men and women of the two parishes to testify to rights which they claimed had been exercised from time immemorial. Photographs of the old folk posing in Devizes Market-place still survive. The rumpus ended in a compromise, each village retaining the use of a footpath to Salisbury.

The records of the Petty Sessions supply much minor information. Here we read of convictions for poaching in the 1840s and 1850s, the names of some incorrigible offenders occurring again and again. One litigious person prosecutes two neighbours for stealing a side of bacon but in the same month is himself prosecuted for stealing a sack of barley. A carter driving a waggon on a turnpike road is fined for not having a second person to lead one of his two horses, thus illustrating a somewhat obscure point of the contemporary law.

The sale of the Ilchester estates in 1912 allowed a generation of small farmers to become owner-occupiers, by taking advantage of the opportunity to buy the farms they were renting. A group of them, however, was unable to raise the necessary funds and so persuaded the Wiltshire County Council to purchase the land as County Council Smallholdings, with themselves remaining in possession as tenants. This state of affairs still prevails.

So we arrive at the threshold of the present day. In this village, chosen for the chance that it happens to be the one I know best, we have been able to trace its development and the shaping of the surrounding countryside from prehistoric times. Here we have the burial mounds, settlements and grassy tracks of prehistoric men. We have a hill-top fortress. The Romans were here, living on their country estates and carving their great roads across the countryside. The Saxons came and formed their humble but tenacious settlements. The marauding Danes passed through in the Dark Ages and left their name as a memorial to their intrusion. The Normans developed the woodlands as a royal chase and laid out a pattern of forest and field which has survived largely to the present time. There are connections with mediaeval saints and Stuart statesmen. The Black Death took its toll; the enclosures transformed the landscape; generations of country people played their part in national and local events which loomed largely in their lives but many of which are now forgotten.

There is nothing remarkable in the story. It is doubtless repeated in virtually every parish in the kingdom. What happened in this village is a microcosm of events throughout the kingdom. A reader can fill into the same pattern the details for his or her own parish. Against that background informed imagination can reconstruct the lives and problems, the triumphs and anxieties, of men and women who lived in whatever period catches our interest.

We will now look more closely at the countryside in and around this selected village in the early years of the twentieth century, with the end of the Great Depression, just before the Second World War, as our demarcation line.

The agricultural land was occupied by eleven farmers, with holdings ranging from about twenty acres to just over ninety. Only three of these farms was in a ring fence. The typical pattern of the others was a farmhouse, farmyard, buildings and one meadow in the village, with other lands distributed around the parish. Most farms had some land on one side of the village and some on another, thus perpetuating the old open-field arrangement by which each farmer had his share of both the good and the bad soils.

In this instance, there existed a practical reason for keeping the old pattern of field distribution. The village was situated in the lowest part of a dry valley and for its water supply was reliant on wells, which were here at their shallowest, though even so one of them was 120 feet deep. For watering livestock there was one public pond and a number on private land, though most of them tended to dry up in a dry summer and were, in any case, highly contaminated. For domestic supplies, and indeed often for consumption by livestock, water had to be drawn from the wells by bucket and windlass, the latter turned by hand.

The farms were mixed smallholdings. Although the tradition in this part of England was of sheep and corn, almost all the sheep flocks had disappeared by the 1920s. Sheep farmers who had clung to the old system of high farming, sound though it was technically, had gone bankrupt in large numbers, wondering what had hit them. Most of the village farms now cultivated half-a-dozen or so arable fields, growing crops of wheat, oats and barley which tended to give steadily decreasing yields. The sheep which should have replenished their fertility had now gone, and the fields were too far from water supplies to be efficiently used by cattle. In the 1920s, as the Depression started to bite deeper, most farms installed a small dairy herd, which at least produced milk for the family and provided a regular income, but the lay-out of the farms was not suited to such an enterprise. At about four o'clock on summer afternoons, five or six herds could be seen plodding in slow procession towards the village from the outlying fields. Each in turn drank at the village pond and dropped their urine and excrement as they drank. No wonder the village livestock was riddled with disease. Milking was by hand in makeshift sheds in the farmyards, for few farms were equipped with proper milking sheds. The dairies were in the farmhouses. The cows were mostly mongrel Shorthorns, with a few crossbred Guernseys and Jerseys; Friesians had not yet found their way into our village. Every farm had a horse or two, two-horse team being the standard, though some farms managed with one horse and others had a spare one. A few farmers possessed a pony as well, for driving to market. One combined farming with market gardening and had a pony and cart to take produce to market. Another had a cattle-cart for taking to market livestock, such as calves and pigs, which were too small to walk.

Horses were the power-unit for work on the land as well as for transport. Some farmers had a double-furrowed plough but most used a single-furrowed one, and one farmer had an old-fashioned wooden plough. Mowing grass in the 1920s was done by a horse-drawn grasscutter, and reaping corn by a binder, but the age of the scythe and the reap-hook were only just past. Most farmers and many farm workers possessed a scythe and were expert in its use. A swathe was mown by scythe around each cornfield before the binder moved in. Sowing was by seed-drill but not by the combine-drill, which sows fertilizer at the same time as seed. Chemical fertilizers were almost unknown. In the 1930s on our farm we began using sulphate of ammonia, spreading it with shovels from the back of a cart. Occasionally we used basic slag and, from time to time, lime. Just before my time, corn was sown by hand, by men striding across the field with a 'seed-lip' containing the grain slung over their shoulder, and I have sown both grain and sulphate of ammonia by this method. It was very hard work.

Haymaking and harvesting were social and communal occasions. Everyone available participated. When mowing by scythe was the normal practice, a woman followed each mower, tying the fallen corn-stalks into sheaves, but in my time the role of women was to bring refreshments to the harvest-field at tea-time, though some helped with the stooking of the sheaves (called 'hiling' in the West Country) or on the corn rick. A feature that had disappeared since the beginning of the century was the practice of gleaning. Throughout the nineteenth century, village women, comprising the wives of farm workers, widows and paupers on parish relief, systematically collected the shed ears of corn in the harvest-fields after the sheaves had been carted away. Gleaning was regulated by rigid rules, such as that which allowed the wives of carters and shepherds to glean between the standing stooks of corn, and was in some districts organized by a formidable dame who ensured that there was no cheating.

Corn ricks were rectangular in shape and were constructed sometimes in groups in the open fields and sometimes in rickyards by the farm. Building ricks was a skilled job and was usually the prerogative of the farmer himself. Some farmers could never master the art, and their unsymmetrical efforts, propped up by poles, attracted a good deal of ribaldry. A rick with a well-made roof would keep out rain for two or three months without thatching, but all ricks expected to survive till the New Year were thatched, some by the local professional thatcher and some by one of the farm workers. The threshing of the ricks occurred at any time during autumn or winter, according to the availability of a threshing-machine and to the farmer's need for ready cash. Threshing-tackle, drawn by a steam-engine on iron wheels, did the threshing on contract, covering the farms over a wide district. When it appeared in the village, most of the farmers tried to arrange to hire it. The threshing 'caravan' consisted of the steam-engine, the 'box' (containing the threshing mechanism), the elevator (for dealing with the straw) and the driver's hut. This last was like a shepherd's hut, a rectangular box on iron wheels containing an old iron stove, a bed of sorts, a chair or two and sundry tools and utensils. The men who manned the thresher saw their homes only at week-ends and were in the meantime perpetually encased in soot, dust and oil. The steam-engine was an innovation; till late in the nineteenth century the thresher was drawn by horses and operated by horse-gear.

Still earlier in the nineteenth century, the introduction of the threshing-machine was the event which sparked off the peasants' revolt in 1830. Ricks were burned, threshing-machines were smashed and the Government, thinking it had a new version of the French Revolution on its hands, was thoroughly frightened. The uprising caused a reversal to the older practice of threshing with flails. Although throughout the century these were gradually superseded by threshing-machines, flails were still in use at the turn of the century for specialist jobs, such as threshing grass seed, and most farms could muster a flail or two and a man who knew how to use them.

All pastures were permanent. Knowledge of the benefits of alternate husbandry, meaning the rotation of arable with grass over a cycle of years, so that the arable crops could cash in on the accumulated fertility produced in the grassland by grazing animals, had evidently been lost. However, temporary grasses were used in the arable rotation for producing hay. The general mixture was of ryegrass and red clover. It was cut in June for hay, sometimes a second time in August or September, then ploughed up for a grain crop. Occasionally such a ley would be left for two years, and then sainfoin would be one of the ingredients.

Most farmers grew an acre or two of mangolds, for the winter feeding of cattle, and some grew turnips and swedes. The turnips were usually eaten in the fields in autumn, but the mangolds and sometimes the swedes were pulled and stored in clamps, thickly covered with straw and then thatched. In winter carting mangolds or swedes for the cows was one of the daily chores. Sometimes they were scattered over a pasture for the cows to nibble; sometimes they were brought to the farmyard, to be sliced by a mangold-cutter and fed in the stall to cattle. Mangold heaps were quite frequently robbed by fallow deer, then plentiful in this district.

Supplementary or concentrated food for cattle consisted chiefly of cattle cake, bought in large slabs, like tombstones, and broken into small pieces by a cake-crusher. Barley meal was also sometimes used, and bran for sick animals and for horses, but ready-mixed concentrates were not known. Now and again a farmer would grow a half-acre of cow cabbages ('broad battises' they were called) on a field of the best land. Potatoes were solely a garden crop.

Agriculture practice here in the 1920s was a makeshift economy, groping its way towards some kind of stability after losing its main props. The sheep-and-corn system, under which flocks of sheep were penned on turnips and other crops grown in arable fields, thus continually renewing the soil fertility, had served the light soils well, and milking-cows were not a satisfactory substitute. Consequently the fields farthest from home were less and less worth cultivating and were falling into dereliction.

In the farmyard itself and the home pasture, most farmers kept twenty or thirty fowls, some more. They were housed in portable wooden houses which, after harvest, were hauled out to the cornfields so that the hens would find their own living on the stubbles. Chicks were hatched from sittings of eggs (thirteen was the standard number) under broody hens, and both cockerels and pullets were retained. The cockerels were destined for the table but were mostly sold, being regarded as too expensive a dish for all but the wealthier farmers. Most farms also kept a few ducks, geese, pigs and sometimes turkeys. All the poultry ran together in the farmyard, scratching for part of their living in the dunghills.

Pigs were a feature not only of farmsteads but also of cottage gardens. The far end of most cottage gardens was adorned by two small buildings – the pigsty and the outdoor privy. Nearby was a rhubarb patch which owed much of its luxuriance to both. Many cottagers kept two pigs, one for home use and one for sale, which helped to pay for any barley meal fed.

November was the recognized pig-killing month, as the ham and bacon could then be cured in cool weather. The village had an official pig-killer, appointed by the village pig club. At some time between the two wars, it became necessary to hire a butcher to come to stun the pig with a humane-killer before cutting its throat, but before that piece of legislation the village pig-killer did what was necessary with his sharp knife. The squealing of a protesting pig being led to sacrifice was a familiar sound on frosty or misty autumn mornings. Thereafter for a week or two the fortunate family who owned the pig feasted on such unaccustomed luxuries as chitterlings, faggots, scraps, melts and black pudding, while the hams and sides of bacons were bedded down in silts of wood or lead and thoroughly salted. The hams and bacon were later hung in the chimney or stored on bacon racks under the kitchen ceiling, for use as required.

Cows being something of an innovation in this village, the disposal of the milk constituted a problem. At first the farm wives made it into butter and fed the whey to the pigs, but in the early 1920s the advent of motor traffic enabled an enterprising villager to invest in a ton lorry for all kinds of transport work, including the daily taking of milk to the town. Individual farmers had to make their own terms with the dairies there and were greatly relieved when the Milk Marketing Board was formed in 1933 to conduct negotiations for them.

The virtual disappearance of the sheep flocks removed many of the features of farm life which were familiar until at least the end of the nineteenth century. Then rural life in the chalk districts revolved as much around the sheep flock as around the cycle of corn-growing. Lambing in February was followed by downland grazing in summer, by sheep-washing and sheep-shearing and by the summer and autumn fairs. The shepherd was the aristocrat of the farm, a perfectionist who put the welfare of his flock first and demanded that the farmer do the same. Shearing was a task performed by itinerant gangs of skilled men (as was mowing in some districts), and many of the villagers found employment in these gangs.

A directory of 1866 catalogues other trades followed by Pitton villagers as shoemaker, wood-dealer, builder and wheelwright, smith, shopkeeper, carrier and innkeeper. The absence of a baker indicates that baking was still being done in cottage ovens, though later in the century a village baker set up shop, delivering bread from a hand-cart. At a somewhat earlier date the village had two limekilns, supplied from the local chalk and operated by a builder. Their remains are still detectable.

The wood-dealer represents a whole stratum of village workers considered to be too insignificant for inclusion in a Post Office directory. These were self-employed workers who gained their livelihood by seasonal work on the farms or in the woods. In autumn they would buy the underwood, mainly of hazel, in one of the local woods and would spend the winter cutting it and fashioning it into hurdles, tool handles, faggots, pea-sticks, ladders and other products. (Some enormous bavins used to be sent to Southampton, as fenders for ships entering port.) In summer they would do contract hoeing or would join a shearing or mowing gang. And they would be on hand to help, on a day-work basis, with the harvest and the threshing. Such casual workers comprised probably nearly half the working population of the village. It was a way of life which appealed to the independent spirit inherited from the old peasant class.

Of the houses in the village, all except two handsome farmhouses (one Georgian, one a fine Queen Anne building) were of chalk cob and flint, with thatched roofs. Farm buildings were of the same material, and so were the cottages. As the 1866 directory reveals no thatcher, presumably the thatching was done by farm workers, though perhaps the thatcher was considered of insufficient status to be included. In the 1920s we had a professional though self-taught thatcher. He used wheat straw grown locally, not imported reed. Chalk cob was a home-made material prepared by mixing rubbly chalk with chaff, horsehair and water to form a kind of paste, which was then thrown into position by flat-grained prongs. Most of the cottages had been built by the villagers themselves (or the ancestors of the current occupants) in their spare time. Many were on odd plots of land by an unfenced roadside, and a group of them clustered on some waste land adjacent to the old limekilns – an uncomfortable and insalubrious spot. Many of the old cottages, some picturesquely half-timbered, still stand and are eagerly purchased by commuters and retired folk for ten times as much money as the builders ever handled in their lifetime.

The old church, reputedly dating from the twelfth century, was a plain, unpretentious edifice which was taken in hand and thoroughly restored in typical Victorian manner in 1878. Tucked away behind it was a Wesleyan chapel, erected about 1840, to replace a cottage that had been used for Methodist services. Apparently there must have been a local feeling for the sanctity of that particular site; the chapel had to be built as near to the church as possible. In 1888 another, larger and more modern brick chapel was built in another part of the village and was for years a focus of village life. Villages tended to be either 'church' or 'chapel', and Pitton, without a resident parson, was a chapel village.

The only other building of any consequence was the school, a Church of England establishment founded in 1853. It provided an excellent basic education for generations of village children, and still, happily, does so.

The village in the 1920s had, of course, no electricity or

telephone. These two amenities, together with a piped water supply, were added in 1938. But between the end of the Victorian era and the 1920s were added two new elements which did little to improve the country scene. One was galvanized iron; the other, barbed wire. Both soon became common features of the village. Corrugated galvanized iron sheets began to replace thatch as roofing material, and rusty sheets of it were employed to stop gaps in hedges or repair pigsties. Barbed wire encouraged the neglect of hedges and threw unsightly barriers across open fields. Both innovations added to the general air of neglect and depression. In Pitton a more commendable feature was the erection of an old wooden army hut, surplus from the First World War, as a village hall, which provided a venue for social activities for the next thirty years or so.

The rim of hills that surrounded the valley was the ultimate horizon for a good proportion of the inhabitants of the village. A carrier's cart made the journey to Salisbury twice a week, on Tuesdays and Saturdays, but was not heavily patronized by passengers. It was used chiefly as a parcel agency, the carrier performing a multitude of commissions for his customers. The aged and mothers with small children would sometimes travel by carrier's cart, but, being a $2\frac{1}{2}$ hours' journey, it was a major undertaking. Able-bodied folk preferred to walk by the four-mile short cut through the woods. Cottage housewives, however, would generally undertake the expedition to town only twice a year – once at Easter or Whitsun, to buy new clothes, and once in October, to attend Salisbury Fair.

Within the village a tremendous amount of intermarrying occurred. Most of the people were related to each other. Typical was a wedding of which I have an account, in which the two brides were sisters, the two bridegrooms cousins, and the brides were cousins to the bridegrooms. Gossip was rife, and small events loomed large. However, new elements of population were introduced by the year-labourers. Several farmers had cottages which went with the job – tied cottages. The workers who occupied them made a contract for a year with the farmer and were at liberty to move on at Michaelmas. Many of them did so, for these were often men with itchy feet, who liked a change of scenery. So a familiar autumn sight in the countryside was a farm waggon laden with all the worldly possessions of a farm worker *en route* to a new job, his wife often nursing a baby and several small children trotting along behind.

The roads were mostly mere cart-tracks, though some within the boundaries of the parish were surfaced with flints. 'Stone-picking' was a recognized and familiar job on fallow fields in summer and was usually performed by old men and women. The picker collected the stones in buckets and made long heaps of them by the roadside, being paid at so much per yard. The local roadman was employed by the parish at a very low wage, but his perquisites included the right to cut the wide verges of the roads for hay. When the County Council took over the responsibility for the roads in the 1920s, many lanes that had formerly been surfaced were abandoned, but the old hard layer of flints may still be detected beneath the mud.

At or before the parish boundaries, the surfaced roads, in most instances, ended. The farther away from the village a road happened to be, the less inclined was the parish council to spend money and energy on mending it. From Pitton the Salisbury road entered Winterbourne Earls parish less than a mile out of the village, whereas Winterbourne village was four miles away, and Winterbourne people seldom if ever used this road. That mattered little, however, for as soon as the parish boundary was passed, the road emerged on to open downland. All around was derelict land, without fences or hedges and clad only in thin turf. A pedestrian, a horseman or even a waggon might leave the track and steer by sun or stars. Most of the downs had been cultivated in Napoleonic times and perhaps even later, but now they were not even grazed by sheep. Some of the fields had been abandoned without having been sown to grass and were now bearing nothing but a meagre covering of lichens, interspersed by tufts of ragwort. The downs, with their islands of scrub, brambles and juniper, were the home of thousands of rabbits, of wheatears, larks and the then common stone curlew. In 1934 230 acres of this land were sold for £750. My father would have bought it if he could have raised £750, but such a sum was completely beyond him. So we rented the land at half-a-crown an acre and paid the rent in rabbits – two thousand of them caught or shot in the first year. Just space out-of-doors.

Horse traffic was quite plentiful on main roads and caused congestion in the towns, but few except local vehicles ever ventured into the remoter villages, of which ours was one. An occasional visitor to Clarendon, entering the estate by the back door; the school inspector on his annual visit; local preachers arriving to preach at the chapel on Sundays. A feature that had vanished by my time but was commonplace when my father was a boy was the workhouse bread-van, which brought workhouse loaves for distribution to the paupers once a week. A widow with three children would receive five shillings and two loaves of workhouse bread a week. Meagre though this subsistence allowance was and poor the quality of the bread, it was better than having to go to the workhouse, which was a permanent menace overhanging the heads of the poor. It was the penultimate destination of old age, before a place in the churchyard – the culmination of a lifetime's hard work. James Hammett, one of the Tolpuddle martyrs who managed to find his way back to Dorset after being released from his term in Australia, resumed work on the land and, when he became too old for further labours, walked over to Dorchester to end his days in the comfortless workhouse there. The workhouses were huge, bleak buildings designed specifically to make them unattractive, on the theory that, if they were objectionable enough, poor persons would do almost anything to avoid entering one. Which was perfectly true, but nevertheless they were usually well populated by unfortunates who had no alternative. Some of the buildings, renovated and modernized of course, still function as old people's homes. Incidentally, for the purpose of administering the workhouses, the Government went back to the old unit of the 'hundred'. Until 1834 poor relief had been a matter for each parish, but by then the burden on the rates had become so heavy that district centres in which indigent paupers could be concentrated ('concentration camps' would have been an appropriate term for them) were felt to be a necessity, and the unit chosen was the hundred. If you became a charge on the rates, you were sent to the workhouse of the hundred in which your parish was situated. It was the longest journey that some villagers undertook in their lives.

Among my earliest memories is travelling to town by

carrier's cart and exclaiming excitedly that we must be getting near because I could see telephone wires. We also passed under a railway arch. The modern age was drawing near, although it had not yet reached our village.

The time was not to be long delayed. Within my memory the first car picked its way along the village roads, and the first aeroplane passed through the skies overhead. I saw them both. What is perhaps even more startling is that my father, in the early 1890s, rode the first bicycle ever to belong in our village, apart, that is, from a solid-tyred penny-farthing bicycle which an old chap bought at a sale. So recent is the revolution in transport which was to pitchfork sleepy old English villages into the modern age.

Above: A village pond – Newton-under-Rawcliffe, near Pickering, Yorkshire. *Below:* Farm-workers' houses built in the early-nineteenth century at Settrington, near Malton, North Yorkshire.

The farm horse. *Above:* Cutting hay in 1941. *Below:* Going for upland hay (to be carried on the wooden sledge) at Dentdale, Yorkshire, in 1955.

Transition to mechanization. *Above:* A threshing machine in operation on Standean Farm, near Ditchling Beacon, Sussex, in 1941. *Below:* Harvesting oats near Melcombe Bingham, Dorset, in 1956.

Modern farming. *Above:* Harvesting near Howsham, east of the River Derwent, North Yorkshire. *Below:* Chisel ploughing.

The new landscape. *Above:* Light industry and uniform housing on the outskirts of Brighton, Sussex. *Below:* The view north along the M6 from Forton Services, near Lancaster.

The countryside for leisure. *Above:* Slapton Ley Nature Reserve, South Devon – a narrow stretch of water, reeds and marsh, separated from the sea by a shingle belt, which attracts a great variety of bird and plant life. *Below:* Village cricket at Patrington, near Hull, North Humberside.

Above: Pleasure-craft at Torksey Lock on the Fossdyke Canal. Dug by the Romans in AD 120, widened and deepened in the Middle Ages, it is Britain's oldest canal still in use. *Below:* A ramblers' path – the South Downs Way above Cuckmere Haven, Sussex.

The townsman's vision of the countryside: a thatched cottage and tidy garden.

8

The Modern Contribution

The long neglect of agriculture brought undeserved dividends
in the Second World War. The derelict fields benefited from
their period of fallow, which had provided an opportunity for
them to replenish, to some small degree, their fertility. But
new factors were now appearing to make their reclamation
feasible.

One was the introduction of mechanical power on the farm.
The first tractor to appear in our village was an iron-wheeled
Fordson which my father bought in 1934. It was the herald of
a revolution.

Probably more important was the introduction and
increasing availability of chemical fertilizers. Much
controversy has raged around the desirability and indeed the
morality of using chemical fertilizers, though fundamentally
all manures are chemical. In practice, they enabled the
remoter fields, which had never been manured by farmyard
manure because of the distance from the farmyard and which
had received no nutrients at all since the sheep had left the
farms, to be cultivated again. Recognition of their value was
slow at first but inevitable. Thin soils on the hill tops which
had been thought not worth cultivating began to produce first
crops of barley and then such demanding crops as potatoes,
wheat and even brussels sprouts. From being useless space
out-of-doors the abandoned fields began to have a new
economic significance.

Reclamation of neglected lands and the recovery of British
agriculture began in the late 1930s but had not advanced far
before Hitler's war struck the country. Thereafter for a decade
or more every pound of food that could be produced from our
home fields was badly needed. In 1939 the proportion of food

imported into Britain was more than seventy per cent. Only thirty per cent was home-produced. This state of affairs needed to be reversed.

Agriculture therefore went on to a war footing, and War Agricultural Executive Committees were set up to direct the campaign. One important action was to offer a subsidy per acre for all old grassland ploughed up and sown to crops. This had the effect of restoring more than $5\frac{1}{2}$ million acres to cultivation by 1945. Yet in spite of the reduction in grassland, milk supplies actually rose by about a hundred thousand gallons a year in the same period. The explanation lay in more efficient husbandry, the use of better cows and the greater productivity of the remaining grassland through judicious manuring.

Towards the end of the war, an increasing volume of farm machinery started to pour into the country from America, under the Lease-Lend agreement. Farmers made the acquaintance of modern farm machinery, not only better tractors on pneumatic tyres but combine-drills (for sowing seed and fertilizer together) and combine-harvesters, as well as new types of harrows, cultivators and barn machinery. And with the combine-drill came the notion of compound fertilizers, in which the basic plant foods (nitrogen, potassium and phosphates) were blended in stated proportions, calculated according to the needs of the several crops. Compound concentrates, applying the same principles to livestock feeding, were also becoming available.

Before and during the war, the gospel of ley farming or alternate husbandry was preached with great effect by Professor Sir George Stapledon. His message was an old one, that the optimum rotation comprised several years of cropping followed by several years in which the field lay under grass. The more intensively the grass was grazed by livestock, the greater the fertility the soil accumulated. Then, after four or five years, the time came to plough in the grass and cash in on that fertility.

The timing was now particularly apt because the ploughing-up campaign of the war years put into practice one half of the theory. Next it was necessary to apply the second half and re-sow the cropped fields to grass, in defiance of the old country proverb that "to break a pasture makes a man; to make a pasture breaks a man". But a new weapon was ready to hand. Sir George Stapledon had served his apprenticeship at the Welsh Plant-Breeding Station which had been established at Aberystwyth in 1919. He himself had done a great deal of the pioneer work in studying and classifying available grasses, from which the Station had bred a new and highly productive range of grasses and white clovers. These could now be blended into a balanced seed mixture to suit every type of soil and climate. The doctrine was so obviously sound and the results so convincing that ley farming quickly became popular. The stage was set for an indefinite continuation of the highly productive farming practised during the national emergency.

In 1947 the passing of an Agriculture Act to protect farming from the sort of depression which had struck it in the 1920s filled many of the older generation of farmers with foreboding. To them it seemed to resemble too closely the Corn Production Act of 1918 which, introduced for the same reason, was repealed with disastrous results three years later. Under the same pressures, they argued, history was sure to repeat itself. They were wrong. The 1947 Agriculture Act remained on the statute book and became the foundation of all subsequent agricultural policies largely because the continuance of the Cold War impressed on politicians the need to be prepared. A contributory factor was the rapid growth in world population, resulting in a greater demand for food by new markets, thus restricting the quantities available for Britain to import.

Two of the main achievements of this Agriculture Act were (a) to establish an annual price review, at which representatives of the Government and the farmers meet to fix minimum prices for commodities for the coming year, and (b) the forming of the National Agricultural Advisory Service. This latter has since changed its name to the Agricultural Development and Advisory Service but maintains its role of providing farmers with technical advice and information.

As the country settled down after the war and rationing of all kinds was gradually abolished, life became less easy for farmers. Pressure to intensify production increased. Instead of twenty cows being regarded as an efficient dairy unit, one man was expected to handle sixty, seventy, sometimes over a hundred. He was enabled to do so by the installation of sophisticated types of milking parlour, operated by a push-button system. Individual cows were carefully rationed according to their milk production, their concentrate rations being calculated to the last ounce and their farm-produced fodder being carefully analysed and scientifically blended with the concentrates. Silage became fashionable, and with it new machines for cutting the grass and making the silage. I saw the first forage-harvesters, now commonplace, at a demonstration in Hampshire in 1958. Tall towers for storing either grass silage or grain began to be features of modern farmsteads, while multi-purpose Dutch barns became an almost essential unit on every livestock establishment. The use of plastic materials was soon widespread, among their chief applications on the farm being polythene sheets for covering silage clamps and heavy polythene or alkathene piping for taking water supplies across fields. Now few fields lack a piped water supply, which, of course, greatly facilitates the efficient use of the land and enables intensive grazing coupled with alternate husbandry to be carried on almost everywhere.

Not all was unmitigated progress, however. The demand for yet more and more efficient production – 'productivity' was the new word coined for it – required still more intensive stocking, till no dairy farmer was content unless his cows were being pastured at less than a cow per acre. The leys were rationed out in daily stints, just as turnips had been rationed to sheep a hundred years earlier, but now the barriers were electric fences, run from a battery, rather than hurdles. Sometimes fields were divided into small paddocks, each of the right size to give a day's feeding to the herd; more often rationing was by strip-grazing, the electric fence being moved every day to give access to a fresh strip of grass (though the system was also used with kale, a crop which became very popular). For this system new grazing strains of perennial ryegrass proved most productive, and so it became the fashion to sow new leys exclusively of this grass and to dress them very heavily with nitrogen after each use (for grazing or silage). The lack of balance in such a diet caused an increase in such ailments as hypomagnesaemia, which was treated by dosing with magnesium and other trace elements. Experiments to determine the best rations for cattle of various ages are still in progress, but there is a swing of opinion towards the belief that a sward of mixed grasses and clover is better than a stand of pure ryegrass. As an aid to a more efficient assessment of rations, many feeding-stuff firms now offer an advisory service backed by electronic computers. Such assistance is in general welcomed by dairy farmers who set their sights on an average milk yield of over two thousand gallons per lactation for their cows. It is a tribute to them and to the veterinary services that the cows so often achieve and surpass that target. They are in far better health than the disease-ridden mongrels of the 1920s. Bovine tuberculosis has been eradicated, and brucellosis is on the way to complete elimination.

Free-range hens, table poultry and turkeys are now exceptional. Most poultry are kept in units of tens of thousands in a controlled environment, meaning vast buildings in which temperature, ventilation and light are carefully controlled and food can be accurately rationed. Laying hens occupy wire cages in endless tiers in battery houses, pecking their food from a moving conveyor-belt in front of the cage. Table poultry, hatched by giant incubators, never see daylight but are killed and dressed when eleven or twelve weeks old. These mass-production methods have so slashed the price of poultry that chicken and turkey are among the least expensive meats in the shops. From being a luxury for special seasons only forty years ago, they have become some of the commonest dishes.

Similar intensive methods have been used with pigs and, to some extent, with beef cattle. Only sheep do not lend themselves to indoor rearing and fattening. They thrive better in the open air, though some of them are grazed at intensive rates on pastures. Sheep farmers also try to increase the lambing average, which means breeding for as many twins and triplets as possible.

Arable farmers in the 1920s used to take as their target a yield of twenty hundredweight of grain per acre. In all but the best farming districts, if they managed to achieve that, they were well satisfied. Now they are disappointed if their crops do not produce at least double that weight, and yields of over seventy and even eighty hundredweight per acre have been recorded. Potatoes and sugar beet have become major field crops, producing a heavy tonnage per acre.

The introduction of the combine-harvester, largely under Lease-Lend towards the end of the Second World War, produced several problems for which farmers were unprepared. They had failed to appreciate the value of straw as a drying agency, in spite of an old saying that it was safe to make wheat sheaves into a rick "when the water ran out of the waggon bottoms", provided the rick was allowed to stand till after Christmas. The combine-harvester threshed as it cut the grain, which in consequence had too high a moisture content for storage. Numerous makeshift devices, such as standing sacks of wheat on end to dry in the open air, were tried until it was realized that an essential accessory to a combine-harvester was a grain-dryer. Now such an installation is standard equipment on grain-growing farms. Often it is combined with a battery of chutes and elevators leading to a series of huge storage bins.

Rick-building has become an obsolete art, apart from a minority of farms which grow crops of wheat for supplying thatching straw as well as grain. Normally the straw is deposited in swathes across the fields by the combine-harvester and is later picked up by a baler. Farms which are exclusively arable, however, have little or no use for large quantities of straw, unless the demand from livestock farms keeps the price up. Their chief preoccupation is to clear the straw out of the way in order to get the land ploughed for the next crop, and the quickest way to do that is to burn it. At the end of harvest, therefore, the countryside in an arable district sometimes looks as though it is experiencing an invasion by Huns, with everything going up in flames in all directions. Even when straw has been baled and collected, the stubbles are sometimes burned, to clear them of weeds.

Hay also is baled nowadays, instead of being built into ricks. Numerous spectacular forms of tedder, for turning and fluffing up hay that is being dried, may be seen in the fields from June to August. Getting the grass adequately dried in the fields for packing into tight bales is a problem in our climate, and some farmers have installed grass-dryers. Farm staff have had to learn the art of stacking bales from scratch, for it is entirely different from making a rick of sheaves or loose material. Most hay, however, is stored in Dutch barns.

What with buildings to house intensive units for livestock,

buildings for storing silage, grain, hay, straw and other crops, buildings housing grain- and grass-dryers and other barn machinery, and buildings for tractors, combine-harvesters and other implements, the modern farmstead is a much larger complex than formerly. Often it covers several acres, the buildings being surrounded by concrete yards and approach-roads, while at the back everything drains into slurry pits or lagoons. Disposing of slurry (farmyard manure mixed with liquid) is a major problem on many farms, though where possible the stuff is pumped over the adjacent fields.

The pressure on storage space is, however, eased by the fact that chemical fertilizers are now delivered in strong plastic bags, each of fifty-six pounds, which can be stored outdoors. Another important factor is the rise of the contractor. Farm machinery now tends to be so big, so elaborate and so expensive that many of the small farmers prefer to hire a contractor to do seasonal work for them, such as harvesting, rather than invest heavily in machinery that will be used for only a few weeks each year.

It goes almost without saying that the modern farm is equipped with piped water, electricity and telephone. As these amenities are so widely available, the pressures that kept the farms in the villages have vanished, and there has been a general trend to move farmsteads that were formerly so situated out into the fields, where they form fortress-like units.

The capital invested in a modern farm of any size can be enormous, but the security to borrow it is usually provided by the land. Farms which changed hands at the price of a few pounds per acre in the 1930s are now worth more than £1000 per acre. A man who bought, or whose father bought, a thousand acres of cheap land forty years ago now finds himself a millionaire, at least on paper. But the money that has been made from agriculture since the Second World War has come from the appreciation in value of land rather than from farming activities. The average tenant farmer has not done so well.

The fears of the labourers of 1830 that the threshing-machines would rob them of their jobs have, of course, been abundantly realized. The labour force of the farms has been falling steadily since the war. Most farms of two hundred acres or less (except in districts of intensive cropping, such as the Fens) are run by the farmer himself, if lucky with the help of his family. On larger farms men are employed at a rate of one man for each hundred to two hundred acres, with specialist employees operating intensive livestock units. Modern farming has ceased to be the social, communal life it once was. The modern farm worker leads a somewhat lonely life, often working in the fields or buildings day after day without seeing another soul.

The achievements of modern British farms are impressive. The British farm worker produces on average enough food for twenty-three townspeople, as against nine for Germany, eight for France and seven for Italy. In some highly farmed districts the record is even better. It has been estimated that the villages of the Deverill valley, near Warminster, produce from their 12,397 acres food to the value of at least a million pounds. Much of this land consists of thin downland soils, on hills rising to over nine hundred feet, which before 1940 was considered not worth cultivating. Each man employed on the big Deverill farms has been calculated to produce food worth around £25,000. Cobbett, when he had recovered from his initial amazement, would have revelled in those statistics, especially as the population of the five villages of the valley is only about eleven hundred, compared to 2,118 a hundred years ago. But the mouths that eat the food produced from the Deverill fields are those of the workers who make the machinery, tools and fertilizers that help to make it all possible – people who live in distant factory towns. An estimate of the money invested in farm machinery in the valley is put conservatively at £250,000.

One further feature of the agricultural revolution which needs to be mentioned is chemical sprays. They are of three sorts, herbicides, fungicides and insecticides. All are developments of well-known garden defences against weeds, pests and diseases.

Weeds have long been one of the farmer's chief enemies. Back in the early eighteenth century one of the prime motives of Jethro Tull in inventing his seed-drill was the urgency of dealing with the weeds which infested the new crop, turnips. By sowing the seeds in rows instead of broadcast, Tull made possible the destruction of weeds by running a horse-hoe (another of his inventions) along between the ranks. However, charlock, which is nearly related to the turnip botanically, remained a major competitor of both root and corn crops until after the Second World War. For more than two centuries, many a farm worker spent the best part of the summer turnip-hoeing. There was even a song written about it. Now a spraying with a selective herbicide is all that is needed to control charlock, which has in consequence become a rather uncommon weed in many districts.

Selective herbicides are those which act on one type, or botanical family, of weeds, leaving others unharmed. They are therefore very useful in killing broad-leaved weeds in corn crops. There are also general herbicides which kill everything they touch but become inert as soon as they reach the soil. One commonly used is paraquat, which is extensively employed in killing off the grass of old pastures preparatory to ploughing. It has made possible a new technique – direct drilling – which means the sowing of seed and fertilizer for a new crop directly into the soil thus cleared, without ploughing it. A special type of combine-drill is required for the job.

The insects which are most damaging to farmers, as to gardeners, are aphids. Unfortunately they tend to attack cereal crops in early summer, when the plants have grown tall. The farmer then has to choose between running a spraying machine through the standing corn and accepting any damage the tractor wheels may do or, alternatively, having the fields sprayed from the air. An increasing number of farmers choose the latter alternative, even although it is expensive. But spraying of all kinds is often done by contractors.

The best-known example of a fungus disease is probably potato-blight, with which every gardener is familiar. The traditional remedy or preventive is spraying with Bordeaux mixture. With cereal crops, much can be achieved by dressing the seed with some toxic substance, traditionally with copper sulphate (blue vitriol), which has now been superseded by more complex chemicals. Other fungus diseases against which spraying is sometimes necessary are mildews and rusts. But credit must be given to plant-breeders, who strive to build resistance to the various diseases into their new high-yielding varieties of farm crops.

Few agricultural developments have aroused more controversy and general interest than the increasing use of chemical sprays. The practice of drenching large areas of the countryside with poisons has naturally caused apprehension and alarm, especially as in some places, notably America, the new technique has been carried to excess. It has to be seen in perspective, as one of the weapons in the farmer's incessant warfare against pests and diseases. Without it, the prodigious demands for food could never be met. And at the moment there is no adequate alternative. A leading American scientist in the field of biological pest-control, which means controlling pests and diseases by means of other pests and diseases, told me not long ago that his great fear was that public demand would compel a reliance on biological methods before he and his fellow scientists were ready for it. Then the method would fail and bring the whole concept into disrepute, whereas, given time, it may eventually be entirely practicable. Meantime, biological pest-control has chalked up some triumphs, notably in America, and even in Britain a build-up of the ladybird population, for instance, will sometimes, though not always, deal effectively with a plague of aphids. Some of the more toxic chemicals have been banned in recent years. They include the organo-chlorines, which are persistent poisons with a chain reaction, passing from one body to another and causing heavy mortality in wild life.

The whole subject is very complex. Although among weeds the charlock menace has been mastered, other weeds, comparatively rare forty or fifty years ago, have become abundant. Goosefoot, redshank and cleavers (goosegrass), which are examples, are weeds which like good living and are indicative of the increased fertility of the soil. Wild oats, now a major menace, have probably been spread with seed corn. The small grey slugs which sometimes play havoc with wheat crops are creatures which thrive in soils rich in organic matter, such as newly-ploughed leys. As fast as each new threat develops, scientists produce a chemical weapon to help fight it. The race is now so fast and furious that not all the new chemicals have their possible side-effects thoroughly studied before they are released on the market. Constant vigilance is necessary.

Which brings us to the phenomenon of the renewed urban interest in agriculture and the countryside.

I have just been examining a selection of the Christmas

numbers of the *Illustrated Times* and the *Illustrated London News* for the 1850s and 1860s and find them as romantic and sentimental as might be expected. Everything speaks of a secure and properly ordered world, on the lines of

"The rich man in his castle, the poor man at his gate,
God made them high or lowly and ordered their estate."

To provide a contrast with the scenes of festivity, the balls, the masques, the charades, the sleek horses drawing sleighs over snow, the papers introduce such scenes as "The Shepherd's Christmas" in a turf hut on Brighton downs, and "The Christmas Dole", depicting a group of paupers waiting in heavy snow outside the ornamental gates of a mansion. The gulf between rich and poor in the countryside was deep and wide; between the industrial workers of the towns and the life of the countryside, it was completely unbridged.

Around the turn of the century, a new generation of writers attempted to introduce the country to the town in terms of everyday life. W.H. Hudson and Richard Jefferies were early pioneers. The farmers had to wait for their champion till the mid-1930s, when A.G. Street exploded into the literary world. Around the same time the BBC was beginning to popularize rural topics.

The war impressed upon the urban populace the almost forgotten fact of how dependent they were on Britain's farms for their food, but the real blending of town and country began after the war. Then the towns discovered the countryside as a place not only to be visited and enjoyed but also to be lived in.

Increased mobility was the key. The motor car enabled the countryman to extend his horizons by escaping more frequently from the restrictions of his native village, but it also provided the means whereby the town could come to him. The country became a place for picnics and holidays, a place for recreation, the lungs of the cities. One of the earliest excursions I can remember as a small boy was, tucked in the rear of a Ford van, to Stonehenge, where we picnicked sitting on the great stones. Apart from our family, there was not a soul in sight, except a distant shepherd with a few sheep. Nor had barbed wire yet invaded the landscape. Now the spacious car park is hardly adequate for the holiday floods of cars, an access tunnel has been constructed under the main road, and the public have now been banned from the immediate vicinity of the stones, not so much for fear of vandalism but because the sheer weight of their feet is wearing away the turf. It lends point to the inspired cartoon of an ancient villager rushing into the inn with the message, "Take to the hills! We've won the prize for the prettiest village in the county!", and in the background are the vanguard of the advancing army of sightseers' cars.

From visiting the countryside on holiday to setting down roots there was a short step. First, attracted by the availability of electricity, telephone, piped water, good roads, in some instances gas and, increasingly, main sewerage, retired people were among the most numerous newcomers. About the same time the country week-end cottage became a cult. Then the feasibility of commuting daily from a village nest began to dawn. By the early 1970s most villages were inhabited mainly by commuters and retired folk. Many of the former were reconciled to spending several hours each day in travelling to and from work. Any village within twenty miles of a town of any size, any village within seventy or eighty miles of London or some other big city, became acceptable commuter territory.

The new residents bought up and modernized such picturesque cottages as the planning department of the local council had not already condemned and demolished. Local landowners sold meadows for bungalow estates, the new houses packed in at eight or ten per acre. In some instances entire new villages sprang up on neglected land far from any existing village centre, though after a time the planning authorities frowned on that procedure and insisted on the policy of 'in-filling', which meant cramming as many houses as possible into the existing limits of the village.

Most of the newcomers belonged to the middle class, of the type which habitually lived in the outer zone of cities. They had preconceived notions of what village life ought to be and did their best to iron out any discrepancies that they found. They tried to shape their new environment to resemble as nearly as possible the suburbs they had left. The word 'suburbage', which I have just coined, describes accurately the new commuter village. The remaining farm workers and other rural craftsmen and artisans have, in the meantime, tended to move into council houses. As a general rule, the new class cleavage in the countryside tends to be between the council house tenants and the rest, though not on any acrimonious terms.

For many, perhaps most villages, the influx of newcomers has been providential. There are so few jobs available on the farms of today that any village totally dependent on agriculture would probably soon wilt and die. Planning authorities usually resist attempts to establish or enlarge village-based industries, on the grounds that villages should be residential and that industries belong to towns. Commendably, independent villagers dig their heels in and insist on developing their industries outside their back doors. In a typical but not imaginary West Country village can be found a small engineering works, a woodworking establishment producing highly-skilled craftsmanship, a bus depot, a small publishing firm, a company collecting waste paper and a little factory for manufacturing components for some piece of electronic gear.

The social life of an alert village is perhaps fuller than ever, with Women's Institutes, clubs for senior citizens, play groups, drama societies and organizations for all manner of sectional interests, according to the leanings of those who have come to settle in the place. Church and chapel have largely, though not in every instance, lost their role as foci of social life. Few villages now have a band, once one of the commonest features of village life, but some have pop groups. There has been a revival of old country pastimes, such as Morris dancing and mumming plays. One deplorable development has been the widespread closing of village primary schools. Many more would have disappeared if public-spirited villagers had not fought hard to keep them. The loss has been disastrous in the many instances where the school has also served as a village hall. Its closure and subsequent sale, often as a week-end cottage, has deprived the unfortunate village of any hope of maintaining a social or community life, no other public buildings being available for any gatherings. It is rather saddening, too, to live in a village where there are never voices of children shouting in a school playground. Even small mites are whisked off by bus to comprehensive schools miles away every morning.

One reason why planning authorities and councils

disapprove of village developments in general is that providing the basic services to villages is much more expensive than to towns. The distances involved often double the costs of such amenities as water and sewerage. Some counties which have got around to studying the problem have more or less convinced themselves that the only way to deal with it, in an economy-ridden age, is to abandon large numbers of villages. People will still be able to live, if they choose, in the villages selected for death, but at their own expense. They will not be able to demand the normal services that a council supplies; the roads will not be mended; letters will have to be fetched from the post office; bus services will cease. So the policy will, if implemented, eventually result in the elimination from the map of rural Britain the names of many Domesday villages.

In these past few pages recreation and amenities have featured quite prominently. They are new factors in the story of the countryside. Far from being merely space out-of-doors, rural land is in strong demand for a multitude of purposes. Someone twenty years ago calculated that if every person and authority with a stake in the countryside were allowed the minimum amount of land which it claimed was absolutely necessary for its efficient functioning, at least four times the total area of Great Britain would be required, and the situation has worsened considerably since then.

Apart from agriculture the main claimants to a share of the countryside are recreation and amenities, industrial and urban development, sport, forestry, motorways, defence and nature conservation.

Of these, industrial and urban development and motorways take a heavy and permanent toll of land most of which can never be restored to the countryside. It amounts to around 50,000 acres a year. The only exceptions to the permanent loss of these acres are (a) land required for opencast coal-mining, which is afterwards restored to agricultural use by well-tried methods, and (b) the grass verges of motorways, which, although unavailable as farmland, are becoming sanctuaries for wild life.

Defence also takes large areas of land from which the public is excluded. That is no bad thing, from the point of view of nature conservation. The two greatest menaces to wild life in Britain, both animal and plant, are the plough and people. An occasional irruption of tanks or the explosion of a barrage of shells has far less effect on a bird and mammal population than has the daily tramping of hundreds of people, no matter how well intentioned. The best nature reserve I know in the south of England is a few square miles of downland and woodland strictly protected by the Ministry of Defence. On the few occasions when I have been permitted past the formidable enclosing fence, I have seen foxes and badgers roaming about in broad daylight, stone-curlews and red-backed shrikes nesting, downland orchids flowering, chalkhill blues and other uncommon butterflies by the hundred and commoner birds and plants in abundance. A cross-section of the wild life once found on all the unploughed downland but now banished by the plough.

Forestry and farming have proved to be compatible neighbours. When the Forestry Commission first began its extensive plantings of conifers between the wars, it aroused considerable agitation, especially in the Lake District and other areas of scenic beauty. In those early days the Commission had only itself to thank, for it set to work unimaginatively, planting firs in rigid rectangular blocks on formerly picturesque mountainsides. Soon, however, it learned its lesson, and later plantings have been models of landscaping, with mixed deciduous trees set as a border around the commercial spruce and fir. When the time came for the first of the early plantations to be felled, there was local opposition of much the same calibre as that which followed the planting of those same trees!

Forestry blends well with rural sport, such as pheasant shooting, and with recreation. The picnic sites, equipped with toilets, barbecue stands, water-taps, tables with benches and other amenities which are such a common and attractive feature of American, Canadian and some European forests, are still thin on the ground, but progress is being made. Nature trails, with maps and signposts, are multiplying. Some of the best forest amenities in the United Kingdom are to be found in the woods of Northern Ireland.

The predilection of the Forestry Commission and private owners of forests for conifers has often been deplored, but commerical demand for timber has switched from oak to softwoods, and forest woodland is a commercial crop. It is needed for pulpwood, planking, pit-props and a hundred other purposes. In the Forest of Rheola in South Wales the trees that supply the pit-props grow on the hills actually over the mines in which they will ultimately be used. In Northumberland sheep farmers on the fells had strong reservations about the planting of forests on their hills, but the trees have proved a useful shelter to the valley lands and have indeed improved their climate.

The two major interests that are least compatible are recreation and nature conservation. The more popular a locality is for recreation, the less attractive it is to wild life. Several hundreds of species of plants are at present threatened with extinction by the sheer numbers of people who invade their habitat. Concern is being felt even for the future of such popular places of pilgrimage as Land's End and the summit of Snowdon, which are being worn away by human feet, much as the approaches to the shrines of saints were worn down by mediaeval pilgrims.

With the contention that farming and nature conservation are incompatible, I would strongly disagree. During my farming days my farm also functioned as a nature reserve. Naturally hedges are valuable refuges for wild life, and their large-scale destruction has been widely condemned, but if modern methods of ploughing demand the elimination of some hedges, the balance may be restored by planting diamond-shaped spinneys and thickets in field corners. The essential is to have cover to which birds, animals and insects can retire.

Much is sometimes made of censuses of birds, which show that in the nesting season broad acres of arable land are virtually deserts. This is true for a few months in the middle of summer, though, in spite of it, such birds of the open fields as skylarks and lapwings manage to thrive. But the censuses ignore the vast numbers of birds which flock to the stubble fields in autumn and feed there during winter. The bare fields are invaluable foraging-grounds.

Nature conservation, however, has become a victim of its own popularity. What an attractive way of earning a livelihood, assuming that is possible! So organizations concerned with the countryside and conservation have multiplied, and with them berths for the boys. Ecology and environment are two of the most fashionable words of the seventies. The entire area has become ultra-scientific and professional, and students of human nature as well as of wild nature will know that any hierarchy or bureaucracy thus formed will excel at finding means to justify its existence and extend its influence. One does not have to be a cynic to suspect that many assertions about the incompatibility of farming and nature conservation, with the corollary that areas for nature conservation should be put under the control of nature conservationists, have ulterior motives.

Nevertheless, there are still innumerable amateurs who take pleasure out of simply observing nature and being in the countryside.

9

Features of the Countryside

FIELDS AND ENCLOSURES

The shapes of fields offer a clue to their origin. *Large rectangular fields* in arable country, surrounded by mainly hawthorn hedges, generally belong to the eighteenth or early nineteenth century and were planned as a result of an enclosure act (see Chapter 6).

Traces of the old *open-field* system, originating in Saxon times, may be detected in parallel corrugations in many fields, especially in what is now meadow-land. They are the strips into which the open fields were once divided and which were allotted to the various peasants and farmers according to status and custom (see Chapter 5). In a few places, for example Laxton and the Isle of Axholme, on the borders of Nottinghamshire and Lincolnshire, the open-field system is still intact. The system is also known as *rigg and furrow*, and the corrugations are known as *baulks*.

In grass country the fields are often smaller and are separated from each other by larger, wider hedges. These probably never belonged to an open-field system but were formed by pioneers carving a farm out of forest, marsh or hill pasture.

L-shaped fields are usually an amalgamation of two fields at right angles to each other.

Triangular fields, or fields tapering to an acute angle, generally represent the odd bit left over when an open field was enclosed and divided. Such fields are usually called *Picked*. On parish maps we find numerous fields with the name Picked Piece, Picked Close, Picked Hill and Picked Croft.

The study of *field names* is a fascinating one. One needs

guidance, for it has its snares and pitfalls. Some names are quite straightforward, such as Swinedale, Maple Close and Bull Marsh, but others are not what they seem. Slaughter Field is derived from an old English word for a sloe tree; Iron Field means 'land in a corner'; Dog Close or Dog Croft is more likely to refer to docks growing on the land than to dogs. Some names carry interesting allusions. Halfpenny, for instance, refers to the halfpenny per beast paid by drovers to farmers for the right to rest their herds and flocks there overnight. Gospel Hill or Gospel Oak denotes a place where the gospel was read by parishioners beating the bounds of a parish at Rogationtide.

Lynchets are long, narrow fields arranged in terraces on hillsides, often one above another in a step pattern. Most of them are Anglo-Saxon or mediaeval, but some may have been constructed during the Napoleonic Wars.

Water-meadows are riverside pastures laid out, in a grid-iron pattern, for irrigation (usually in winter against frost, in order to produce good grazing early in spring). (See Chapter 7.)

Croft is the name now usually given to a smallholding in the Scottish Highlands. Traditionally they were little farms of fifty acres or less, and usually only a few acres belonged to the crofter, the rest of the holding consisting of grazing rights on the surrounding hills.

In-bye land relates to mountain or hill farms in Scotland and northern England. It is the name given to fields enclosed, usually by a stone wall, on the sloping land above the farmstead.

Lazy-beds represent a method of growing crops on poor, thin or boggy hill-land. The beds, about six feet square, are built up of soil, farmyard manure and/or seaweed. Their name indicates that they can be cultivated without digging, by men working from paths alongside.

Common land is land over which the local community has rights, usually strictly defined. It is usually unfenced and uncultivated. It does not, however, belong to the public in general, and no rights of access should be taken for granted.

Parks are enclosed but generally uncultivated land, mostly pasture but with a scattering of trees. They were originally reserved for hunting by kings or nobles. After the enclosure acts, many were laid out, by skilled landscape artists, as pleasure-grounds around country mansions. *Urban parks* have, from the mid-nineteenth century onwards, been designed for recreation of the populace in general. *National Parks* are large areas of picturesque and attractive countryside to which the public has access for walking and other quiet recreations.

Orchards are enclosures devoted to the growing of fruit trees. Apples, plums and pears are the most numerous. Most of the older orchards are of standard trees, but the newer ones are generally of bush trees, which are planted closer together and start to produce good crops at an earlier stage.

Activity Patterns in Fields

It is interesting to note in the fields the patterns that denote seasonal farming activities. When cutting corn with a *binder*, a farmer would drive his machine round and round the field, making a concentric pattern. The sheaves would be picked up and stood in stooks or hiles, to dry, making similar concentric rows. Most drivers of *combine-harvesters* follow the same practice, though it is not strictly necessary, as do men mowing grass with a grass-cutter. Drivers of *hay-tedders* and *balers* naturally have to follow the swathes of hay or straw, thus creating a similar pattern.

For traditional *ploughing*, the ploughman marks off a headland, around the margins of the field, and then divides the rest of the field into sections, or *rudges*, which he ploughs one by one. In working down the soil to a fine tilth for sowing in autumn or spring, the farm worker uses a variety of implements, including the *cultivator, harrows* and *roller*, each of which forms its own pattern across the soft earth. Normally each cultivation is at right angles or at an oblique angle to the previous one. The *combine-drill* follows when cultivation is finished and forms a pattern of narrow, shallow rows over the surface of the field. This pattern becomes clearer when the seed starts to sprout, and any mistakes the worker has made are also revealed for all to see! Drilling is usually carried out in parallel lines across the field, not in concentric circles.

Grass cut by a *forage-harvester*, for taking to livestock or for making silage, is usually cut in strips, across the field; and grass rationed out for *grazing* by means of an electric fence is also allocated in strips, as are, generally, kale and roots.

Potatoes are planted in furrows, the furrows being then

reversed to form ridges halfway up the potato plant.

Fallow land is land given a rest from bearing a crop for an entire summer. Traditionally it is kept cultivated from time to time, in order to suppress weeds and admit sunlight and air. Few farmers today can afford to allow a field to remain idle for a whole season, however.

Erosion is not a serious problem in most of Britain. It can occur when hillsides are ploughed and cultivated, for heavy rain will wash the loose soil downhill, carving out gullies. It can also occur in the form of drifting soil, blown by the wind. This second type of erosion does sometimes happen on the light soils of the Fens and East Anglia. A 'blow' will occasionally shift the top inch or so of soil across the field and deposit it in the boundary ditch.

Archaeological Field Patterns

Cultivations and weather conditions quite often reveal otherwise hidden archaeological features. For example, on bare fields in the chalk country the outlines of ancient fields, buildings and trackways are visible through lighter markings, due to the shallowness of the soil. In times of drought, similar patterns are revealed in grassland, the grass over the foundations of walls having shallower roots which are thus more susceptible to lack of water. On the other hand, former kitchen middens are marked by a more luxuriant vegetation.

Field markings are most easily detectable from the air, and aerial photography has been a potent aid to modern archaeology.

FENCES AND BOUNDARIES

Hedges are the traditional form of fencing over most of lowland Britain. The Midland hedge, it was said, had to be strong enough to fence in a bull. Hawthorn is one of the best bushes for hedge-making and was very extensively employed for fencing in the new fields formed as a result of the enclosure acts.

Traditionally, a hedge is only one part of a boundary barrier. It should be accompanied by a *ditch*. The hedge is on the land of the owner whose property it protects; the ditch is on the far side, protecting the hedge from damage by a neighbour's cattle. Quite frequently hedges may be found with a kink in them. Closer investigation will show that where the kink occurs, the ownership of the hedge changes. The ditch is in a straight line but the hedge crosses it from one side to the other.

The hedge is a living barrier. When the bushes which compose it are from one to three or four inches in diameter at the base, their trunks are slashed half-through just above ground level, and the bushes are then bent over at an oblique angle – all at the same angle, so that the stems are lying parallel to and on top of each other. Straight stakes of an inch or so in diameter are then driven into the ground at intervals of about two feet, and the bushes are woven around them. The weaving is so ordered that the twiggy tips of the bushes are always directed inwards, on the opposite side to the ditch, and are left untrimmed. They thus form a kind of thorny outwork, deterring livestock from approaching the heart of the hedge and trying to force their way through. The shape of the hedge as well as the position of the ditch is thus a clue to the ownership of the land. A well-laid hedge has its woven bushes kept in position by a top layer of some very supple wood, such as hazel or even brambles and briars, closely plaited around the stakes.

The composition of hedges is a rough-and-ready clue to their age. *One species of bush to a hundred years* can be taken as a general rule, though requiring some elasticity. Thus, hedges of the enclosure age were usually of pure hawthorn when planted, but many of them have now been invaded by another species or two. Those which have not been properly maintained can generally show a few elder bushes, which are a useless hedging material. In my native south-country village, the hedges of an area of small fields, marked on an early-nineteenth-century map as "ancient enclosures", are composed of six species of woody plants, excluding brambles and briars. They are hawthorn, blackthorn, hazel, holly, maple and oak. This mixture would indicate a fourteenth-century date of origin, and a study of other evidence seems to render that most likely. Cottage hedges in villages often harbour a few species of plants indicative of considerable antiquity. Hops and periwinkles are examples. The sites of former cottages may sometimes be detected by observation of hedge species.

Old photographs show some cottage gardens and small fields in the vicinity of villages fenced by *dry hedges*, or *woven hurdles*. Such hedges are of necessity only temporary, as they decay through exposure to the weather, and hurdles today are too dear for extensive use, though they are sometimes employed on a small scale in suburban gardens. A few farms still use woven hurdles for making temporary sheep folds (as described in Chapter 7).

Rail fences of split timber have also become rather rare. They must once have been common but declined in popularity with the increasing scarcity of timber. Shortage of wood in even what were once well-forested districts reached such a stage that a common offence in the eighteenth and early nineteenth centuries was the robbing of hedges for firewood by cottage housewives.

The great estates of the enclosure age surrounded themselves with formidable and impressive barriers of whatever local material was most easily available. *Precinct walls* of stone and brick several miles long were quite common, and *iron railings* were extensively used. The latter were also frequent features of village and suburban gardens, but many were sacrificed for scrap metal in the Second World War.

Barbed wire is a twentieth-century innovation which has done nothing to enhance the beauty of the countryside. A well-made barbed wire fence is efficient when properly maintained though bleak in appearance, but a neglected one which has started to sag and has been patched by the insertion of additional posts is one of the worst of rural eyesores. Even more unsightly is the use of barbed wire for blocking gaps in hedges and other fences, as also is the detaching of a section of barbed wire fence to form a gate. Modern barbed wire fences, particularly alongside motorways or protecting Ministry of Defence establishments, are often of six or eight strands of wire (as against two or three in normal farm fences) and are anchored by concrete posts, which look impressive but are easily broken by a sudden hefty blow.

For internal field divisions and for keeping livestock away from badly maintained hedges and other barriers, *electric fences* are now extensively used. They are operated by portable batteries. For keeping sheep and pigs within bounds, fences of *plastic mesh* are coming into fashion, and some of these are electrified.

In stone districts the place of hedges and barbed wire fences is taken by *drystone walls*, which are stone walls made without mortar. In Scotland they are known as *dry stane dykes*. The difference is one of name, but drystone walling shows a considerable variation of type, according to local tradition and the available stone. Some are capped in one way, some in another; some have through-bands, or horizontal layers of wider stones at intervals, some have not. Nearly all are wider at the bottom than at the top, and all owe their durability to the skill of the craftsmen who made them.

Although drystone walling is a very ancient art, most of the walls that mark field boundaries were constructed, like quickset hedges, in the age of enclosures. Many of them are as sound today as when they were built, though much depends on keeping the coping intact. Once the coping stones are pushed off, the wall soon starts to disintegrate.

In many districts drystone walls are combined with *earthen banks* and hedges to form composite and highly efficient barriers. The hedges of Cornwall and Devon are of this type, so is the similar Galloway hedge. Often these hedges are on sloping ground, with the level of the field inside the barrier higher than that outside. Then the bushes often take root on the inside of the wall and force their way through it to form a hedge on the outside. But in Devon and Cornwall the bushes grow on the wall, in it and all around it. Banks of earth or turf are a natural barrier, still to be seen on the northern Scottish moors, where trees and even bushes are scarce. Elsewhere the natural sequence of events is for the earth bank to be reinforced by either bushes or stones or both.

The difference between the earthen bank with which the crofter surrounds his home plot and the earthen ramparts which were the basic defences of prehistoric hill-forts is merely one of degree. And, as already noted (see Chapter 2), some of the earliest of hill-forts probably began life as cattle corrals. As with traditional hedges, they were protected on the outer side by a ditch. Probably those which served as cattle enclosures were surmounted by a hedge or fence, the latter of timber or wattle-work. For military defence, the earthen rampart was, one supposes, crowned by massive walls, first of timber and later of stone. Where possible, the ditch around the rampart was filled with water, to form a moat. To visualize such a fort or castle as it once was, requires an effort of the imagination, for centuries of British weather have caused the soil and rubble that covered the slopes to slip downhill, so that the incline is less steep and the ditch less deep than they once were. When in use, the ramparts would probably be bare of soil and would look stark and formidable, especially in the chalk country, where they would be dazzling white. The great dykes which traverse miles of countryside, such as Offa's Dyke on the borders of Wales, the Wansdyke in Wiltshire, and the Devil's Dyke in Cambridgeshire, probably presented a similar appearance and may well have been crowned by some subsidiary defence-work.

In drained marshland, the *ditches* and *canals* serve as water boundaries to fields. From a distance, a marsh landscape may appear to consist of flat meadow-land, without barriers, but a pedestrian who tries to make his way across it will find himself thwarted by a series of deep, water-filled ditches, in many instances too wide to be crossed without a bridge, as the Duke of Monmouth discovered on a fateful day in 1685 at Sedgemoor. To anyone unaccustomed to such a landscape, the numerous gates erected apparently haphazardly and without flanking hedges or fences are a curious and bizarre feature. Each gate guards the approach to a separate field, usually over a small bridge:

The *five-barred wooden gate* is a traditional feature of British farms. Five bars is a convenient number for a gate of three or four feet high, which is the usual size, though there are some six-barred and a few four-barred gates, and the cross-bracing pattern varies from district to district. Oak is the favourite wood for a gate, because it is so durable. It should be fastened together with oaken pegs, not nails. Field gates are generally hung on strap hinges and are heavier at the hinge end. If you *must* climb over a gate, always do so at the hinge end. The normal width of a farm or field gate is nine or ten feet, which used to be the right size to admit farm waggons and other machinery. Modern machinery, however, is in many instances too wide for the traditional gates, many of which have therefore had to be demolished. Some have been replaced by gates of tubular steel but more by portable fences, either wire or electric.

Gate-posts, too, are conventionally of oak. The part of the post buried in the ground is generally equal in size and certainly in weight to the visible section. In stone country, gate-posts are often upright stones, with holes drilled to take the hinges. Field gate-posts can repay attention, for occasionally one may be found that started life as a Celtic cross or a pillar in a Roman villa.

Gates in the countryside were for use by vehicles; for pedestrians *stiles* were adequate. The two essentials of a stile is that it admits the passage of people but prevents the passage of animals. Some stiles achieve this by being too narrow for a cow, a horse or even a pig to pass; others require the pedestrian to climb over the barrier by means of several steps; there are also 'cuckoo-cages', which are gates set in a semi-circular frame too narrow for a four-legged animal to negotiate. Stiles have many traditional regional forms which can make an interesting study for a part-time countryman.

A modern barrier designed to be a substitute for a gate is the *cattle-grid*. It consists of a series of parallel bars, usually of tubular steel, laid over a shallow pit extending over the entire width of the roadway. It must be flanked by a strong fence, preventing livestock from creeping around the outside. Its purpose is to allow the passage of motor traffic without the necessity of the driver climbing out to open and shut a gate.

Country roads were made for country traffic. Except where their line was dictated by other features, such as by canals and drainage channels, they tend to be irresolute and meandering, as G.K. Chesterton observed. In general, the older the road, the more sinuous it is, probably because it follows a former cattle-track which bypassed such obstacles as a fallen tree or a boggy puddle. Roads made to serve the fields created by an eighteenth- or nineteenth-century enclosure were usually straight, with junctions at right angles. Few of these were surfaced, and many are still muddy tracks, but generally they are satisfactorily wide. Originally the track itself was narrow but possessed a wide grassy margin on either side, which modern road-makers have been quick to incorporate when it has suited them. Turnpike roads (see Chapter 6) are usually straight though often quite short. Considerable stretches of

Roman roads are incorporated in the modern road system, especially where they saw interim service as coach-roads.

Footpaths were originally entirely utilitarian. They represented a short cut across country between two villages, two groups of cottages, or to the nearest alehouse, church or other much-frequented feature. Originally they were ephemeral, formed by a tired countryman appreciating the shortest distance between two points. After the age of enclosures, many of them became rallying-points for villagers hanging on grimly to what remained of their ancient rights. Latterly they have served to provide ramblers with welcome access to the countryside and have been augmented by long-distance footpaths, such as the Pennine Way and the footpath which extends the entire perimeter of the south-western peninsula.

The name *Harrow-way* applied to a country road implies that the track is very ancient, for 'harrow' is the equivalent of 'hoar', or 'old'. Where they traverse hill slopes, they are usually hollow ways as well as harrow ways, for the passage of vehicles, livestock and pedestrians for many centuries has worn them into a deep hollow. Often such a well-worn track will be flanked by a series, more or less parallel, of similar tracks. These arose from the natural practice of switching to new ground on one side or another of a road that had become impassable through mud or ruts. The tracks would later be deepened by rain water.

FORESTS AND WOODS
Ancient Trees and Forest Vestiges

Most of the deciduous woods and forests surviving in Britain are the vestiges of the primaeval forests which covered the greater part of the island. In most instances, however, they have been tamed for commercial usage. Enactments from the reign of Edward IV, in the early 1480s, permitted the enclosure of sections of forest in order to allow the natural regeneration of the woodland, it being recognized that cattle and pigs wandering freely were destroying the young trees which ought to be the future forest. Some earthen banks and ditches in old forests may well be of this date. Well-managed forests in the seventeenth century were already being laid out in 'walks', each walk being under the control of a single forester, with an interlocking system of broad 'rides'. These rides later provided ideal stands for the guns when shooting pheasants.

Some ancient trees, now isolated, testify to a wider extent of former forests. Of British trees, that which attains the greatest age is the yew, of which the oldest specimen in Britain is said to be the Fortingall Yew near Aberfeldy, Perthshire, probably at least fifteen hundred years old. Oaks are often credited with great age, but as their natural span of life is 250 years, it is unlikely that any have reached three thousand years, as is sometimes claimed. *Gospel trees*, generally Gospel oaks, derived their name from the custom of reading a passage from the Bible under them when beating the bounds of a parish at Rogationtide. A large tree was a useful boundary mark.

The word '*coppice*' is ultimately derived from the Norman-French '*couper*', 'to cut'. Its application to open woodlands is that the young saplings were cut off just above ground level and allowed to shoot out again to provide a new crop of poles, which were used for fencing, building and other country purposes. The practice caused the tree to produce a jagged cushion of wood from which a whole group of saplings, rather than one trunk, would sprout. The species chiefly involved were oak, hazel, sweet chestnut and ash. In many parts of the country, the custom was to grow coppiced hazel or ash under a thin canopy of standard oaks. The coppice thus produced one short-term and one long-term crop.

Coppiced woods provided an important source of livelihood for nineteenth-century villagers. The custom was for the estate-owner to offer for sale the *underwood* in coppices when it had attained its commercial optimum, which ranged from about seven to twenty years, according to species. The purchaser would then cut all the underwood in the approved style, clearing brambles and weeds as he went, and would make the rods and poles into various articles for which a local demand existed, such as hurdles, ladders, thatching-spars, hop-poles and sheep-cribs. A further account of this trade is found on pages 99 & 139. A few underwood workers still operate, current demand being mainly for ornamental hurdles, though in Kent, Sussex, Hampshire and Herefordshire hop-poles of sweet chestnut are still required.

A woodland craft which is now almost extinct is *charcoal*

burning. The few practitioners who survive now use bins of galvanized iron for burning the wood, rather than making the traditional airtight heaps of logs. Memories of old-time charcoal-burners linger, and in some districts a countryman will claim to have seen 'colliers', which are the bluish wisps of smoke from the charcoal-burners' kilns, rising above the tree-tops on calm autumn days, but they are really clouds of gnats dancing.

Coverts often occur in coppices but are sections of woodland in which the underwood is not cut and from which brambles and other undergrowth are not cleared. The vigorous growth of bracken, bramble and other plants which results makes ideal cover for woodland creatures, such as pheasants, deer and foxes. In many woods various bushes have been planted in times past to assist the process. Most of the dense rhododendron thickets which are common in many British woods owe their origin to planting for this purpose.

A *pollarded* tree is one which has had its top cut off at from six to fourteen or fifteen feet above ground. The idea is to encourage the tree to produce a regular crop of young poles or rods for farm and manufacturing use. Cutting the top at a considerable height above ground rather than at ground level as with coppiced trees gave the young shoots a chance to grow without damage from deer. The trees most commonly pollarded were, or are, willow, elm, hornbeam, oak and ash, though almost any deciduous tree may be so treated.

A curious development of tree pollarding was once prevalent in parts of Devon. A large tree was kept pollarded and the young shoots trained horizontally to form a kind of platform. On festival days a platform of planks was erected on this base, a flight of steps placed in position, and festivities were held on it. In some instances the tree was reserved for dancing, the Cross Tree at Moretonhampstead having room "for thirty persons to sit around and six couples to dance, besides the orchestra". In others, tables were laid on the platform for a feast, and a family of tenant farmers at Great Fulford held their land on condition that they dined once a year on the top of the tree. The flat-topped trees were usually oaks or elms.

A feature of the landscape planning of the enlarged estates formed as a result of the enclosures was the *shelter-belt*. While it had the effect of providing useful shelter for arable and pasture land, it was planned with the needs of game as the prime consideration. It introduced coverts into mainly arable and therefore open areas and also created a barrier over which driven partridges were compelled to rise, thus affording a better target for guns. The earlier shelter-belts were often of deciduous trees but later ones – and many were planted right through the nineteenth century – were frequently of conifers.

Hill-top clumps were planted on the highest points of their estates by eighteenth- and nineteenth-century landowners and are still conspicuous landmarks. They are usually of beech, though some are of pine.

Avenues, as approaches to country houses, came into fashion in the seventeenth century; then, after a period of eclipse, they became very popular in the late eighteenth. The early examples were usually of deciduous trees, notably beech, lime, elm, sycamore and horse chestnut. Those planted in the nineteenth century made use of a wider variety of species, including cypress, wellingtonia and other conifers.

Commercial forestry in the present century has needed, by the law of supply and demand, to concentrate on conifers. Very large areas of trees have been planted since the formation in 1919 of the Forestry Commission, which is now responsible for about three million acres of woodland. Some have been on ancient forest land, but others have constituted entirely new forests, such as the breckland forests of Norfolk and the vast new Forest of Kielder in Northumberland. While conifers predominate, most new forests have an uneven margin of deciduous trees and bushes, to enhance their scenic value.

At several places around the coast, the vestiges of *submerged forests* may be seen. The tree trunks, usually of pines, were growing about eight thousand years ago, when the sea level was lower than it is today. As the climate changed, the tree trunks became buried in peat, which preserved them, and then in sand. Now from time to time the sand is washed away on certain beaches, as in Pembrokeshire, East Sussex and Lincolnshire, revealing the remains of the ancient forests.

WATER FEATURES
It is hardly an exaggeration to claim that nearly all human activities in the countryside are dependent, to some degree, on

water. The first settlers (apart from the few who were here before the Straits of Dover were breached) arrived in this country by water. The Anglo-Saxons penetrated by rivers into the heart of England and pitched their settlements by river banks. Those who moved away from these lifelines needed to settle by lakes, ponds or wells to ensure a supply of water for their daily needs. The Normans used water defensively, in the form of moats. In mediaeval times, water turned innumerable mills. Excess water was drained off to open up the Fens and other marshy areas to cultivation. The highways thus created for water-borne traffic in due course initiated the canal age. Water-meadows constituted an early form of irrigation. And today it is said that at least one-third of all sports and recreations are water-based (angling is the most popular of all, surpassing even football in the number of its addicts).

The use of rivers for driving *water-mills* has become obsolete with the passing of the village miller. His disappearance from the country scene has been a fairly recent event, for many country mills were still operating in the 1920s and 1930s. Now milling has become big business, run by the great milling companies, though just a few local millers have retained their independence.

The winter irrigation of riverside meadows has been fairly fully described in Chapter 6 (pages 117-118). This system, too, has become nearly extinct, though a few *water-meadows* are still maintained in working order. Most fell into disuse in the Depression, and when agriculture eventually emerged from that long eclipse, almost all of the old experts, the 'drowners', who knew how to manipulate the system, were dead. Moreover, managing a water-meadow called for a good deal of hand labour, and the operations could hardly be mechanized – a fatal flaw in a machine-obsessed age.

Modern *irrigation* is achieved by means of piped water directed through sprinklers or spray guns. It is expensive and so is usually reserved for high-value crops, such as potatoes, though also on intensively-used grassland. Some farmers employ their irrigation equipment for spreading liquid manure rather than pure water.

The *farm pond* was a variable asset to the countryside. Ponds situated in remote places, for the use of cattle and sheep, were an ecological godsend. Ponds situated in farmyards were more often cess-pits and a source of disease. Natural ponds, fed by springs, are usually ancient, and often the adjacent village has grown up around them. Other ponds accidentally made have resulted from depressions in quarries and brickworks filling with water.

Of man-made ponds the most celebrated example is the *dew-pond*, often found on hill-tops and so-called because it was supposed to be replenished by dew. Modern research has shown that the contribution made by dew is negligible. The pond is kept filled by rainwater draining into it. In the regions in which most 'dew-ponds' are found, the average rainfall is about thirty inches annually, and the evaporation rate eighteen inches. That leaves a surplus of twelve inches per year. Now an inch of rain falling on a surface of a hundred square yards (which would be a fair average size for a pond) deposits 466·5 gallons of water, so there is an annual surplus of 5,598 gallons. That alone would be adequate, but the pond-makers improve upon it. They heap up the excavated material around the perimeter of the pond and so increase its catchment area. A small increase in diameter means a lot more water. Suppose, for instance, that the pond of a hundred square yards has sides of ten yards. Surround it with a margin of three yards, sloping down to the pond, and the catchment area is increased to 256 square yards. The surplus of rainfall over evaporation then amounts to 13,995 gallons per year. Work it out for yourself. The pond is thus sufficient to supply all the drinking water a flock of 130 sheep will need in a year, allowing a hundred gallons per sheep. So much for 'dew-ponds'.

One of the most important aspects of pond-making is the construction of an impervious bed. For this there are many recipes, with clay, puddled chalk, pitch and sometimes a layer of straw as favourite materials. Modern ponds will be of concrete or polythene sheeting. In time the pond either silts up or the bottom wears through. The maximum length of a pond is about 150 years. But many ponds have been re-made many times, so some are undoubtedly ancient.

Other ponds, in valleys, are sometimes fed from rivers and/or springs, as was a frequent arrangement with mediaeval fish-ponds, with which most abbeys, monasteries and other ecclesiastical establishments were well provided.

Some still survive, as do sections of ancient moats around castles and farmsteads. Hammer ponds are features of the Weald and other parts of southern England and were constructed to provide power for iron-smelting. Rivers or streams were dammed to form quite large ponds, from the outlets of which the water turned mill wheels to operate heavy hammers. Again, many traces remain.

The *damming* of streams or rivers to make a pond or lake is a time-honoured device. The principle is employed for mills, irrigation, flood-control and a number of other purposes. The vogue for landscape planning in the eighteenth and nineteenth centuries saw the construction of many new *ornamental lakes* by throwing an earth dam across a convenient brook that happened to traverse a park. Such lakes are still among the most attractive features of both country and urban parks and are highly attractive to waterfowl.

Mediaeval towns drew their water from wells, but as their population increased, it became necessary to bring water from *reservoirs* situated outside the town limits. Perhaps the earliest of such reservoirs in Britain, after the Roman era, was the Westcheap Conduit, which brought water from Paddington to London and was constructed in or just after 1285. The nineteenth century was the great age of reservoir construction, but the work has continued to the present time, as demands for water continually increase. Modern reservoirs are lined with concrete, but even if they have completely bare banks, they attract very large numbers of waterfowl and wading birds, especially in winter and during the migration seasons, and are favourite haunts of ornithologists.

The Scottish Highlands, with their mountainous terrain, deep valleys and high rainfall, are eminently suited to the production of *hydro-electricity*. Scores of great dams from which falling water is harnessed to supply electricity to more than fifty main power-stations span Highland valleys. The reservoirs behind the dams enhance rather than detract from the scenery, and specially constructed salmon-ladders conduct migrating salmon past the barriers to their spawning grounds.

An account of Britain's *canals* is found on pages 119–120. Their ascendancy as a mode of transport for heavy loads came to a fairly abrupt end when railways were built. Many fell into disuse, and many were deliberately closed by railway companies which bought them up in order to stifle competition. Within the past two or three decades, however, they have experienced a revival, though for pleasure rather than utilitarian traffic. Many canals are now thronged with holiday-makers in summer. In a recent year the British Waterways Board issued over twenty thousand licences and permits for pleasure-craft on its canals, and more than two hundred tour-operators offer holidays on inland waters. Around sixteen hundred miles of canals are still navigable, and enthusiasts are constantly working to increase the total by restoring derelict reaches. But even the neglected canals have a high value for the naturalist and conservationist. The means by which a canal is taken over a hill is a system of *locks*, which enables a boat to move uphill by what is in effect a stairway of water. At Tardebigge, in Worcestershire, the Worcester and Birmingham Canal is raised 217 feet in $2\frac{1}{2}$ miles by a series of thirty locks, the largest series in Britain.

An activity which has changed the face of the countryside by many of our larger rivers is the excavation of *gravel*. This is, or was, commonly found as an alluvial deposit in or around river-beds and is in great demand for making concrete. Worked-out gravel-pits normally flood, to create new lakes, for which there is nowadays considerable competition. They naturally attract waterfowl and other birds in great numbers, but they are also in increasing demand for various water sports, such as water-skiing, sailing, canoeing, power-boat racing and angling. Some of these would seem to be mutually exclusive, but schemes for reconciling them are being concocted, with some success. The 3,100-acre Empingham Reservoir, in Rutland, has been planned from its very inception as both a nature reserve and a recreational centre. With picnic areas, trout-fishing, space for sailing over a thousand dinghies, nesting islands for wildfowl, eight miles of footpaths, and ample parking space, it should, when finished, serve as a model for similar schemes in the future; and all these amenities do nothing to hamper its prime purpose of supplying 65 million gallons of water a day to Midland cities.

BUILDINGS
The centre and focus of most villages is the parish *church*. This

book is not the place for a lengthy discourse on ecclesiastical architecture; we will content ourselves by saying that only a very few churches are of Saxon date. The years following the Norman Conquest were a great period for church building, and much Norman work, characterized by its massive piers and rounded arches, survives, though often in churches which have since been extensively rebuilt. Many churches of more recent date retain their Norman font. Church-building was likewise a popular mediaeval activity, the style changing gradually from the massive Norman to the more graceful Early English and then to the light and airy Perpendicular. Private chapels were added to many mediaeval churches at later dates, much of the space in them being occupied by tombs of the benefactors. The interior of village churches usually offers some kind of commentary on the history of the village, featuring crusaders' tombs, structural alterations to meet changing fashions, marble or brass monumental inscriptions, and, in documentary form, lists of rectors or vicars and, from the seventeenth century onwards, the parish registers and churchwardens' account books (though the last two are now more generally kept elsewhere than in the church chest). With little of our own well-developed sense of the value of antiquity, our ancestors cheerfully demolished old churches to make way for more pretentious ones, erected to God's and their own glory. The tendency was most pronounced in Victorian times, when great numbers of parish churches were 'restored', but it was not confined to that era.

In many, perhaps most, parishes, the religious life of the community is shared between the Anglican church and the *nonconformist chapel* (or chapels). The latter buildings are generally utilitarian, uncompromisingly rectangular and plain but often quite well designed for their purpose. The oldest nonconformist chapel in England is at Horningsham, in west Wiltshire, erected for the use of Scottish masons engaged in building Longleat House in 1566. Some chapels, such as early ones of the Baptists and Quakers, are to be found on sites remote from villages, in deference to the Five Mile Act of 1665, which forbade preaching or teaching, other than that of the Established Church, within five miles of a town or city. Some of these older chapels have their own graveyards.

In some villages the parish church stands at a considerable

distance from the main group of houses. In such instances it is usually the village which has moved. The original village would have been in the immediate vicinity of the church, but in the course of centuries the older houses will have been demolished and the village centre developed on a new site, perhaps that of a former hamlet.

Churchyards, like the interior of churches, provide information on the past inhabitants of the village, though after two or three centuries tombstones exposed to the weather tend to become indecipherable. In times past the churchyard and the church porch were the focus of much village life and the scene of fairs, markets, auctions and many sports. Most churchyards have a collection of trees, among which yews are most prominent, especially in southern counties. The theory that they were planted to provide wood for longbows is now generally discounted, but their original purpose is still a matter of some controversy. The main entrance to a churchyard and hence to the church is often guarded by a *lych-gate*, which is a gate protected by a roof and often containing a bench or seat. Its purpose was to provide a resting-place for a coffin and mourners while awaiting the arrival of the priest.

The *rectory* or *vicarage*, adjacent to the churchyard, is often a spacious building of the eighteenth or nineteenth century and speaks of the time when the parish priest was regarded as a minor member of the aristocracy and had a sufficient income to pay for a staff of servants. Far too large for most present-day clergymen, it has in most instances been sold off as a residence to some more affluent household, the priest now occupying a modern and more modest home nearby.

The *country house* or *mansion* has already been dealt with (see pages 100-101). The countryside has examples of all types, from early and mediaeval castles and manor houses to neo-Gothic effusions erected by Victorian tycoons. The stately homes built by the gentry of the eighteenth and nineteenth centuries are the most numerous. Some are still occupied by the families for whom they were built, but many others have changed hands and now serve as hotels, schools and conference centres.

Some of the ancillary features of the great country houses have considerable interest. The enclosures of the eighteenth century were, as we have seen, accompanied by a passion for impressive landscape planning, which was characterized not only by an orderly lay-out of rectangular fields, shelter-belts and coppices but by the erection of architectural features purely for their scenic value. Many a country park has mock Greek temples, ornate bridges over artificial lakes, man-made grottoes and secluded summerhouses in expensive marble. A *prospect tower* on the highest point of an estate was a favourite device. As one landowner of that competitive age remarked, if he couldn't build a bigger house than his neighbour, he could at least erect a tower on an elevation that enabled him to look down on his rival. Such *follies* are numerous. Ornate *gateways* were also in vogue, the little rooms at the base of the great arch on either side of the road serving a secondary function as the residence of the gatekeeper. Yet another feature of the home park was the *ha-ha*, which is a wall with its top course at ground level but its base protected by a deep ditch. It was usually constructed around the home park, in front of the great house, in order to give the residents an unobstructed view of the countryside while keeping livestock out of the garden.

Farms and *farmsteads* present a similar chronological pattern to that of the country houses, except that they have not been so strongly influenced by fashion. Especially in districts of good building stone, many farmhouses and their satellite buildings are centuries old. The great estates of the eighteenth and nineteenth centuries, however, tended to build farmhouses like lesser mansions, to match the architecture of their own houses. In farmhouses of Victorian times, the parlour was a room for use on Sundays, everyday life being lived in the spacious kitchen. The dairy and wash-house were usually annexes, and often the unmarried employees slept in a loft over either the kitchen or the stable, taking their meals with the family.

What are now termed *cottages* are in most instances village houses built for the smaller farmers and for artisans such as carpenters, smiths, weavers and innkeepers. Most of the surviving examples have now been modernized to a degree which would make them virtually unrecognizable to their original owners. The cottages of an earlier age were flimsy constructions that were little more than hovels. The early Anglo-Saxon invaders made their first homes under their upturned boats, and early cottage architecture followed a similar design, with no upright walls but a hut of wattle and daub fashioned around timbers shaped like a Gothic arch. A common complaint in the disturbed years after the Black Death was that peasants absconding from their manors pulled down their houses and took the materials with them, for rebuilding elsewhere. In woodland districts timber was freely used until it became scarce; the half-timbering which we so much admire originated as a concession to sheer necessity. Similarly, thatch, now a rich man's luxury, was once the cheapest form of roofing available to a cottager.

Many cottages owe their origin to squatters. It was generally held that if a man could erect a cottage, complete with chimney, and light a fire on the hearth, between sunset and sunrise, he could thus acquire squatter's rights and could not be disturbed. Many cottages are built on narrow strips of land filched from the road or the edge of a field or wood. Until cottages became desirable rural residences, chiefly after the Second World War, a typical cottage would have one 'front room', one living-room, possibly a back lean-to as a wash-house, and a separate building as a privy alongside the pigsty at the bottom of the garden. At one gable end the thatch would reach down almost to ground level to cover a shed, used for storing wood, onions, tools and other accessories. Sometimes the thatch formed wide eaves under which benches could be placed for bee-hives and flower-pots. The bread-oven was often a brick annexe, built outside the cottage wall but against the chimney, so that it could use the same flue.

The old concept of *farm buildings* was the sensible one, still common in much of Europe and in Scotland and the North, of housing everything under one roof, including the human population. That way the husbandman could move from house to cattle byre without venturing out-of-doors in bad weather. Hay, straw and other foodstuffs were stored in lofts above the cattle stalls. The essential machinery, apart from ploughs and other simple equipment which could be left under a hedge, was housed in a lean-to against the main barn.

Threshed grain was stored in *granaries* usually built on staddle-stones, to keep away rats and mice. Much grain, however, was stored in the sheaf, in readiness for winter threshing. Some of the mediaeval *barns* erected for this purpose are still standing, and functioning, and are noble examples of farm architecture. Some are lofty buildings of stone, with many bays, but the essential feature of all of them is a central threshing-floor with doors on opposite sides of the building, so that a loaded waggon could enter through one doorway, unload into the bays on either side and pass out through the other doorway without turning. Later barns, often of board on a timber frame, were built to the same pattern.

Some of the old barns are large enough and sound enough to be adapted as modern grain stores, with a series of bin siloes linked with a grain-drier and unloading pit at one end. Other farms, not so well-favoured, have to erect new buildings, usually of the *Dutch-barn* type, to house their storage bins.

The modern *farmstead* is a very extensive complex of building, often occupying an acre or more. Surrounded by concrete yards and roads, it contains grain-driers and siloes, covered yards for housing cattle, milking-parlour and dairy, tower siloes for grass silage, machinery sheds and workshops, and intensive, purpose-built houses for units of hundreds of pigs and thousands or tens of thousands of poultry. Well-planned drains lead to huge slurry pits, from which the effluent is pumped to the fields. To a considerable degree, the modern farmstead has returned to the old ideal of housing everything under one roof or, at least, in a concentrated area.

The *portable houses*, each containing from thirty to fifty hens, which were once fashionable poultry units, are not now much used except for rearing stock, though some farmers put both poultry and pigs out on free range. Some wheat, harvested in sheaves for thatching, is still stored in *ricks*, but straw is collected in *bales* which are stored in sheds if there is space available but outdoors in large stacks if not. *Plastic sheeting* is used as a covering. In market garden districts, *glasshouses* are now generally concentrated in large blocks and are heated by electricity or oil rather than steam, as in Victorian times. From the air the island of Guernsey appears to be half-covered by glass. Plastic *cloches* have also become a conspicuous feature of fields in horticultural districts.

Some formerly important features of the agricultural countryside have now become obsolete. *Oast-houses*, for drying hops, are an example, though they were confined to the hop-growing parts of the country, notably Kent, East Sussex, Hampshire, Herefordshire and Worcestershire. Other non-agricultural kilns also made their mark on the countryside, such as *brick-kilns* and *lime-kilns*. As local industries, these were often small and numerous. The chalk country is studded with old *chalk-pits*, from which chalk was dug for spreading on the land, either in its original form or, after burning, as lime.

Many villages still possess a village *smithy*, though the smith is now usually a specialist farrier or combines his blacksmith work with agricultural engineering. Outside in the smithy yard can frequently be found, buried in nettles, and old iron *wheel-binding base*, where formerly iron rims were fitted to the wooden wheels of horse-drawn vehicles. *Cider-mills* were generally portable contraptions which have long since disintegrated, but in some stone districts the big stone vats used in the process can still be seen in farmyards. Purpose-built stone *dove-cots* are a reminder of the long-obsolete practice of keeping doves and pigeons for food (generally for killing as squabs or nestlings). Some of the best examples, as in the Cotswolds, are splendid examples of rural architecture. In some instances a dove-cot will be found incorporated into another building, such as a house or even a church.

In potato-growing districts, the margins of fields are often lined with long *clamps*, sometimes thatched and sometimes earth-covered, but clamps are not nearly as common a feature of the countryside as they were when almost every farmer grew mangolds and stored them in thatched clamps for winter use by cattle.

MISCELLANEOUS FEATURES

An *adit* looks like the mouth of a cave but is, in fact, the entrance to an old mine, entered by a level or sloping path rather than a vertical shaft. Many still exist in mining districts, especially in hill country.

Barrows, or tumuli, are prehistoric burial mounds. They are of several types, of which long barrows and round barrows are the most important. The long barrows are the oldest, belonging to the period roughly 3,000 to 1800 BC. There are over twenty thousand tumuli known in the British Isles.

Bench-marks are incisions in the shape of a broad arrow

topped by a horizontal line which are found on isolated stones in hedge-banks, in walls, churches and other convenient places. The horizontal line marks the exact altitude above sea level, and the appropriate reading may be found on a large-scale Ordnance Survey map.

One of the oldest *bridges* in Britain is the prehistoric Tarr Steps on Exmoor. This is a clapper bridge, a primitive type consisting of flat boulders placed on massive piers of similar up-ended stones. Bridge-building vied with church-building as a pious exercise for rich mediaeval merchants. Many fine mediaeval bridges are still in use. Bridges with houses on them were commonplace in the Middle Ages, Old London Bridge carrying rows of houses and shops five storeys high, and Pulteney Bridge in Bath still has shops upon it, though this last is an eighteenth-century construction. Many mediaeval bridges were designed for packhorses only and so are too narrow for vehicular traffic. Some of the eighteenth- and nineteenth-century bridges erected by turnpike trusts still carry notices advising that vandals will be punished with transportation.

The oldest stone *crosses* were mostly erected by early Christian missionaries to mark preaching-places. Often in Celtic areas, notably Cornwall, they were sacred stones of a previous religion, adapted for the new creed. Celtic crosses usually have the cross surrounded by a circle. Mediaeval crosses were also erected at preaching-places, such as at cross-roads, village centres and market-places, and some were boundary marks. Many survive, often surrounded by stone steps which have been worn hollow by generations of feet. Northern crosses tend to be lavishly decorated with intricate carvings of strange beasts, showing Danish or Norwegian influence.

Dene-holes are remarkable bell-shaped caverns dug into the chalk in southern and eastern England, usually entered through a narrow shaft at the top. Their purpose is unknown, and theories range from refuges from Danish raiders to prehistoric flint-mines. Some were later taken over for other uses, one at Royston having apparently served as a place of worship or as a cult centre, perhaps for Templars. Dene-holes are sometimes found in connected groups.

Gibbets are a kind of gallows, on which the bodies of

criminals were hung after execution as a warning to others. Some are still extant, though renewed from time to time, as, being of wood, they weather quite quickly. They were usually erected on a conspicuous hill or by a well-used road. Inkpen Beacon, at the junction of Berkshire, Hampshire and Wiltshire and one of the highest points in southern England, has a well-known and maintained gibbet.

Hill figures, carved usually on chalk hillsides but in some instances on hill slopes with other subsoils, are prominent features of many southern landscapes. Horses are a favourite subject. The only undoubtedly prehistoric white horse in Britain is the Uffington White Horse, in the Vale of the White Horse in Berkshire, which is probably a tribal totem. Of the eleven white horses in Wiltshire, only one, the Westbury White Horse, has any possible claim to antiquity, but it was probably cut in the eighteenth century, as were most of the others. Cerne Abbas, in Dorset, has a celebrated giant, with prominent phallic features, which probably represents a prehistoric god, the counterpart of the Greek Hercules. Sussex also has a hill figure of some age in the Long Man of Wilmington, which may represent a Saxon god or a mediaeval pilgrim. A range of hills by the A30 road in southern Wiltshire is decorated with a series of regimental crests, mostly carved during the First World War.

Landslides occur around the coast from time to time, as eroded and undermined cliffs collapse into the sea. In the course of time the chaos of rock and soil under the cliffs forms a very interesting ecological habitat. Good examples are to be found in the Undercliff near Ventnor, Isle of Wight, and at several places on the Dorset coast.

Maypoles were once ubiquitous features of the May Day revels in English villages. These festivities were prohibited under the Commonwealth and never generally revived, although some places resurrected the old customs. In recent years there has been a further revival. Maypoles were usually tall poles of hawthorn wood, though sometimes of some other tree, erected on village greens as a focal point for dances. They are supposed to have had a fertility significance and to be a relic of prehistoric worship.

Milestones, with the distances to the nearest towns and to London carved on them, mostly date from the Turnpike Act of

1766, which required their erection. A few Roman milestones survive.

Mines make a mess of the landscape chiefly through the waste they deposit in tips, which frequently assume formidable proportions. Although the operational parts of coal-mines are for the most part out of sight underground, in a coal-mining district the tips entirely dominate the scenery. Until recently they have been uncompromisingly unsightly, but lately attempts have been made to render them less objectionable by covering them with a layer of soil and planting with trees. The results are encouraging.

In *opencast mining* the entire top strata of rocks are removed to expose the coal measures beneath. The coal is then scooped out with heavy machinery, and when the supply is exhausted, the overburden of rocks, the subsoil and the topsoil are replaced in the proper order, having been stored separately. After efficient restoration, the soil is no worse than when the opencast working began and in some instances has been actually improved. While in progress, however, opencast workings are hideous.

Abandoned *tin-mines* of Cornwall are marked by the ruins of engine towers, in which were housed the huge pumps that kept the mines drained. Similar derelict buildings, many of them with tall chimneys, mark the sites of other old mines from which in the eighteenth and nineteenth centuries, and in some instances earlier, copper, lead, zinc, silver, fluorspar and other minerals were extracted. Often they are associated with vast heaps of spoil and sometimes with dangerous holes where the mine ceilings have collapsed. Such vestiges of past industry are particularly plentiful on the Pennines and in the Lake District.

China clay workings are a conspicuous feature of the landscape in east Cornwall and Dartmoor, where the enormous conical heaps of spoil are locally known as the 'Cornish Alps'. They are the refuse from the process of china clay or kaolin extraction. The kaolin, in the form of a fine white powdery rock, is washed out from opencast workings by means of high-pressure water hoses.

Obelisks are tapering towers erected usually on a hill-top to commemorate an important event or some prominent local worthy. Most belong to the same period as the *follies* already mentioned, and some may be considered as such.

In former times most parishes possessed a *pound*, which is a small enclosure in which straying animals were penned until released on payment of a fine and the cost of any damage for which they were responsible. The official in charge of a pound was known as a 'pinder'. In lowland England most pounds, having been made of timber fencing, have disappeared, but northern counties have many pounds enclosed by durable stone walls.

Pylons are a modern and highly conspicuous feature of the scenery. They are an essential part of the national grid which carries electricity across the country.

Quarries may be described as opencast workings for stone. Quarrying has been carried on from time immemorial, some of the older excavations dating from Roman and pre-Roman times. Many of them, such as the slate-quarries of North Wales, cover hundreds of acres. Quarrying is still a live industry, and the extraction of immense quantities of rock by efficient modern machinery makes heavy demands on our land area. One of the most flourishing aspects of quarrying is the extraction and blending of limestone and clay to form cement. Unsightly though they are when in operation, quarries quickly become interesting nature reserves when abandoned.

We have already noted how the *railways* altered the face of Britain in the middle years of the nineteenth century. Deep cuttings, viaducts, bridges, embankments and tunnels transformed the Victorian landscape, much as the motorways are doing in our own age. Now, as many old railway lines fall into disuse and dereliction, they become havens for wild life, many penetrating into the hearts of cities.

The numerous *roundhouses* found in villages or market towns mostly served the specific purpose of lock-ups. It was here that drunkards, beggars and other persons who made a nuisance of themselves were temporarily confined. Some were designed for overnight occupation by prisoners on their way to the county assizes at some distance from the place where they had been arrested. Most of the surviving roundhouses are of stone, and many are of interesting design.

The *sewage works* that now serve most towns and villages are usually of particular interest to ornithologists, for they attract numbers of birds, especially waders, on migration.

Villages and towns used to have a legal obligation to provide *stocks* in some public place, where prisoners could be confined and exposed to the ridicule of passers-by. Although stocks have not been used as a form of punishment since the 1840s, many are still in existence and are now carefully preserved.

Standing stones were regarded with superstitious reverence by our prehistoric ancestors. Many surviving stones are natural formations, but many others have been erected by men. *Menhir* is the name given to a single standing stone. A stone slab resting on two or three upright stones (and usually forming an ancient tomb) is known as a *dolmen*. A circle of standing stones is called a *henge*; hence Stonehenge. Megalith means, simply, 'great stone'. Where, as at Stonehenge, two megaliths support a third resting on them horizontally, the group is known as a *trilithon*.

Some erect stones standing in the middle of fields may be merely rubbing stones, placed there by farmers for cattle to rub against. On the other hand, they may once have served another and perhaps sacred purpose, as have more than one stone gatepost in Cornwall and other stone districts.

Rocking stones are natural formations, the result of erosion by rain and wind.

Cairns are heaps of stones, usually erected on the summit of a hill or mountain. Some are modern and are still being added to, but others are prehistoric and may mark a tomb.

10

The Future of the Countryside

Does our survey of the shaping of the countryside from the earliest times to the present day enable us to indulge in any valid predictions of the future?

We can, I think, detect one axiom controlling almost all of the major changes that have affected the countryside in the past. With the exception of the Black Death and other similar epidemics, all have had a political origin, accepting war as a branch of politics. The invasions that changed society in prehistory, the Roman interlude, the Saxon settlement, the Danish irruption, the Norman Conquest, the Reformation, the enclosures, the long agricultural depression, all were basically political in origin. Someone, somewhere, made a political decision and so set in motion events the effects of which were profound.

In this respect, nothing has changed. The decisions which will affect the countryside in the next fifty years will be mainly political, as those in the past have been. What are they likely to be?

Cataclysmic changes tend to be sudden and difficult to predict. War, invasion or a Communist take-over with a subsequent collectivization of agriculture fall into the category of events impossible to foresee. But, given a continuation of the present political background, it is possible to detect trends.

Over the past fifty years, commercial and social developments in America have tended to find their way to Britain in the course of a few years. It is therefore legitimate to ask what developments affecting agriculture and the countryside are occurring in America today. Being fairly familiar with both the USA and Canada, through having one of my children resident in each of those countries, I feel competent to suggest an answer.

The members of the earliest urban communities continued for a time to be farmers. They had to be, until their economy was sufficiently developed to ensure a steady supply of surplus food to be brought in from the surrounding countryside, thus allowing the urban craftsmen and others to specialize and to forget the obligation of raising their own crops. Even today in the new cities of Africa, administrators, lawyers, politicians, clerics and others of the sophisticated élite still like to keep their roots in the soil; they retain their *shambas* in the rural countryside and even raise crops of maize in the back yards of their elegant villas. When investigating the state of French agriculture just after the war, I was surprised to receive from an Angevin dairy-farmer the following reply to a question about whether the milk he was producing went to Paris:

"No, let the Paris people produce their own milk!"

He was merely expressing the old tradition that every town was surrounded by an agricultural and horticultural belt which supplied it with food.

The concept is still valid for many parts of the Old World. In Britain it has been modified to some extent first by the ultra-rapid growth of some many large new towns in the Industrial Revolution and then by the conquest of the problem of distance by the railways and latterly by modern road transport. The great cities now draw their food supplies from the regions best suited to the production of the various commodities, as, for example, milk from the West Country, brussels sprouts from Bedfordshire, plums from the Vale of Evesham, cabbages from Ormskirk, sheep from the fells, fat cattle from the fattening yards of East Anglia and so on. In most districts, however, a market garden zone still persists around the towns, though nowadays the traffic is two ways, townsfolk coming out in cars to fetch produce from the farm gate as much as the producers bringing their goods into the town for marketing.

From my observation, that state of affairs is unknown in much of America and Canada. The western cities with which I am most familiar do not have a market-garden belt. Housewives buy from the supermarkets which are supplied from whatever sources on the continent are best suited to the production of the various commodities. Distance is no object.

Thus, in a town where I stay on Vancouver Island, most of the vegetables and fruit in the supermarkets are brought up from California. Indeed, the Imperial Valley in southern California, a highly productive region with an ideal climate and adequate irrigation, produces most of the vegetables required in the United States and much of Canada.

The same process is well under way in Britain. Not only do we now draw our supplies of wheat from the American and Canadian prairies and much of our meat from the plains of Australia, New Zealand and South America, but increasing quantities of fruit, vegetables and even flowers are imported from Mediterranean and African countries, and even, as a matter of fact, from distant California. Some British horticulturists are already feeling the squeeze. Growers of early strawberries in sheltered districts in the south-west, for instance, are abandoning their traditional crop in the face of competition from imports from countries with a more favourable climate.

This trend is proceeding with the European Economic Community still in its infancy. When the Common Market becomes fully integrated and its organization completed, the development is bound to accelerate, especially if new countries with a Mediterranean climate, such as Greece, Spain and Portugal, are brought in.

The political decision that will then face the Government of the day will be to what extent to allow Britain to become dependent on outside sources of food rather than from our own fields. Much will depend on its assessment of the danger of war and possible blockade. To what extent shall we need to maintain a reasonably flourishing home agriculture as an insurance? Some will maintain that this is absolutely essential; others will take the opposite view and declare that we might as well let the lot go, for all the use it would be in a nuclear war. The ultimate decision is likely to be, in true British tradition, a compromise.

Ever since the late 1930s, politicians have been exhorting British farmers to become more efficient. The stick-and-carrot methods used to encourage efficiency should, one would think, have eliminated the inefficient farmers long ago, but we shall hear more of the same cry. And two types of farmer will be able to survive the pressures.

One will be the company farmer operating on a very large scale. He will be backed by ample capital resources, controlled through a limited company and maybe even, like the beef-fattening feedlots of America, raised from the general public through the issue of shares. Such an enterprise will be able to employ a staff of specialists, from accountants to veterinary surgeons, and will use the most sophisticated modern machinery and technical devices.

The other will be the family farmer, the eternal peasant. He will survive on his few acres by keeping his overheads low and living largely on his own produce. It will be difficult for him at times, but no one is more tenacious and resilient than the true peasant, and my guess would be that he will still be there when even the big company farms have disappeared.

Now, the peasant will continue to farm just wherever he happens to be. The big commercial farms, on the other hand, naturally need the best land. They will not want to make a heavy capital investment in second-rate stuff. It is not difficult to foresee, therefore, the abandonment of more and more marginal land and even some of the better soils by agriculture. In particular, vast areas of hill land in the west and north may well be vacated by farmers.

In Chapter 8 we took note of the pressures on land by various interests. The withdrawal of farming from much of the countryside would greatly ease the situation. One can visualize that much of the released land would be set aside for recreation and conservation. The family farms that survived in these regions could augment their income and perform a useful service by taking in bed-and-breakfast clients and selling fresh produce to holiday-makers.

Let me stress that this is not a pattern of development that I would advocate. It is what I foresee as a very likely course of events. And it is, in fact, no more than a logical projection of present trends.

There is, however, one trend which I would very much like to see reversed. The take-over of agriculture by big business, with the exception of the family farm, is probably inevitable. It is already well advanced. As it proceeds, the agricultural population of the countryside will diminish still further. Already in most villages the surviving farmers and farm workers are heavily outnumbered by newcomers. The village has indeed become a *suburbage*.

Almost all the newcomers are either retired folk or commuters. They travel every day to their work in towns, sometimes for considerable distances, using their private cars and burning up, incidentally, vast quantities of petrol. Their children, too, are collected daily by coach and taken miles away to schools geared to mass production. A village is a place to relax in, a place to sleep in, but not a place to work in.

This development is likely to spell the ultimate doom of many a village and to accelerate the depopulation of the countryside. Already we see it beginning to happen. Councils have become aware that the provision of sewage disposal plants, refuse collection services, piped water supplies and bus services are far more expensive for the thinly populated countryside. It would be much more economic to bring the village population into the proper suburbs rather than allow them to live in these outlying settlements. And already decisions are being taken to withdraw support from selected uneconomic units. If people choose to live in these remote rural places, they must make the amenities of fresh air, green fields, big gardens and pleasing rural surroundings compensate for the lack of public transport, road repairs and other services of which they will be soon deprived.

The situation might be altered if the countryside were allowed to develop naturally, without official interference. It should be remembered that the purely residential village is a modern phenomenon. Until the 1920s and 1930s, people lived in villages because they worked there. The main rural industry, agriculture, has ceased to be a major employer of labour, and many of the ancillary ones, such as work with underwood and similar crafts, now have little significance. New industries to replace the old are needed.

Many are available, and where these have managed to establish themselves, usually in the face of determined opposition, the villages concerned continue to be vital entities. At present, the obstacles are formidable, for the local councils and planning authorities join forces with the *suburbagers*.

The latter have an instinctive resistance to change. After all, they loved the countryside with the ardour of a true lover –

they loved it just as it was when first they saw it. That is why they moved into residence. Secure now in their modernized 'cottages', they would like to preserve it unchanged and 'unspoilt' for ever. They resist even further residential development, while any suggestion to introduce a factory – even a nice, clean one – is anathema.

Apart from the fact that many local councillors and planners are themselves *suburbagers*, officially they see eye to eye with their neighbours about the undesirability of industrial development in the countryside, though they are primarily motivated by considerations of economy. More development of any kind means more services and more expense, and they have to find the money.

So any attempts to make the countryside once again a kitchen and a workshop rather than a parlour and a bedroom are uphill work.

We must set this somewhat gloomy prognosis, however, against the positive aspects of modern suburbage. Newcomers to village life can legitimately challenge, "Who runs whatever social functions there are now in the countryside? We do!" In many instances that is true. Social life and recreation naturally tend to be more sophisticated than in the old days – with drama groups instead of mumming plays, classes in flower arrangement and the making of corn dollies rather than sheep-shearing parties – but there can be no doubt that the infusion of new blood into the villages has the effect of widening considerably the horizons of those whose families have been static for generations. As ever, it is the women who take the lead. Commuting husbands, reconciled to long journeys to work every day, have little time or energy for social life in the evenings, but wives often have a surplus of both. And no contemporary rural organization is more important or more effective than the Women's Institutes. Generalizations are always invidious, but it is probably true that the social life of most villages is as active and vital as it has ever been. It does, however, tend to be largely a female preserve.

Aesthetically, the prospect of a rural Britain in which very large areas are devoted to recreation and conservation instead of to agriculture is not unattractive. Nor would there be any necessity for the complete exclusion of farming from the hills. Cattle and sheep could continue to graze there all the summer long, before being transported to the eastern lowlands for fattening. Independent peasant holdings would form oases of human activity in national parks and would offer accommodation, food and refreshment to those who came visiting. The mass production of livestock for the supermarkets is already concentrated into buildings which take up comparatively little space and can be concealed by careful landscaping. As for the thousands of acres which would fall derelict, in the agricultural sense of the term, the history of the present century has shown that they can be regarded as a reservoir of fertility, to be tapped in times of emergency.

My mind skips back to the years between the wars, when so much land had been withdrawn from agricultural use and land was indeed 'space out-of-doors'. I remember the snows of winter, when often the sunken lanes which gave access to our village were blocked by drifts for a week or two at a time. I remember the coming of spring, when we took Sunday afternoon walks along those same, traffic-free lanes to pick blue and white scented violets from the hedge-banks. The coppiced woods were spangled with galaxies of primroses, one of which would from time to time take wing and flutter away, to reveal itself as a brimstone butterfly of identical colour to the flowers. The chiffchaff shouted its monotonous song; then swallows twittered back from Africa, and all the meadows resounded with the cuckoo's call.

I remember the scent of hay in early June, and the song of the nightingale by moonlight as we trudged home from the hayfields. The shearing of the sheep, and the hatching of the spring crop of baby chicks and ducklings. The communal marathon that characterized the harvest, and the flood of relief and triumph when the last sheaf was hoisted to the rick and the long battle won. The harvest festivals; the Michaelmas fairs; the beginning of the endless cycle of ploughing and sowing again. The swallows and martins collecting on tiled roofs, in the days before telephone and electricity wires were available; the haunting chorus of dozens of stone curlew carolling together in the autumn twilight. Picking mushrooms when pearly sheets of gossamer swathed themselves around our boots as we waded through the saturated pastures. The closing in of the diminishing autumn days that heralded the programme of social events to fill the dark evenings.

The pageant of the seasons remains, and always will. The primroses will always bloom in the countryside in spring; the swallows will always come in April, when the lambs in the meadows are reacting to the increasing strength of the sun. There will be bluebells in May, nightingales in June, wild thyme and clover in summer, starlings flocking after midsummer, lapwings and swallows in autumn, redwings and fieldfares drifting in as winter looms.

But mingled with these eternal manifestations of nature are other memories of the countryside which I miss. Frosty mornings in winter were enlivened by the shouts and hammerings of men wheel-binding – hammering the heated iron bonds on the cleaving wooden frames of cart-wheels. The smithy was a magician's cave, filled with the scents of glowing fire, the parings of horses' hooves and sweaty leather. The scents of the various woods in the carpenters' shop were fresher but no less distinctive. I miss, too, the sound of bat on leather and the flavour of cricket teas in the cricket season – how few villages now run a cricket club!

The sounds and sights of human activity. And especially of men working and producing something and achieving something. They have become rarer in the modern countryside. Am I being merely nostalgic in longing for their return? Or are they not a vital and integral part of a healthy and vigorous countryside?

Bibliography

Arnold, James, *The Shell Book of Country Crafts*, 1968
Atkinson, R.J.C., *Stonehenge and Avebury*, 1959
Bettey, J.H., *Rural Life in Wessex*, 1977
Blythe, Ronald, *Akenfield*, 1969
Bouser, K.J., *The Drovers*, 1970
Boyd, A.W., *A Country Parish*, 1951
Burton, S.H., *Devon Villages*, 1973
Churchill, Sir Winston, *A History of the English-Speaking Peoples*, 1956
Darley, Gillian, *Villages of Vision*, 1978
Darling, F. Fraser, *Natural History in the Highlands and Islands*, 1947
Donaldson, J.G.S. and Frances, *Farming in Britain Today*, 1969
Edlin, H.L., *Trees, Woods and Man*, 1956
Edlin, H.L., *Woodland Crafts of Britain*, 1973
Enmon, E.A.R., *Adventurers Fen*, 1949
Fairbrother, Nan, *New Lives, New Landscapes*, 1970
Finberg, Joscelyne, *Exploring Villages*, 1958
Fleure, H.J., *A Natural History of Man in Britain*, 1951
Forrest, Denys, *The Making of a Manor*, 1975
Fowler, P.J. (Ed.) *Recent Work in Rural Archaeology*, 1975
Fussell, G.E., *Farming Technique from Prehistoric to Modern Times*, 1966
Gardiner, Rolf, *Water Springing from the Ground*, 1972
Hammond, J.L. and Barbara, *The Village Labourer*, 1911
Hartley, Dorothy, *Made in England*, 1939
Harvey, Nigel, *A History of Farm Buildings*, 1970
Hole, Christina, *English Custom and Usage*, 1941
Hoskins, W.G., *Provincial England*, 1963
Hudson, W.H., *A Shepherd's Life*, 1910

Kenchington, F.E., *The Commoners' New Forest*, 1944
Kerridge, Eric, *The Farmers of Old England*, 1973
Lea, Raymond, *Country Curiosities*, 1973
Marples, Morris, *White Horses*, 1949
Richardson, John, *The Local Historian's Encyclopedia*, 1974
Savage, Derek, *The Cottager's Companion*, 1975
Seebohm, M.E., *The Evolution of the English Farm*, 1952
Seymour, John, *Companion Guide to East Anglia*, 1970
Shepherd, Walter, *The Living Landscape of Britain*, 1962
Stamp, L. Dudley, *Man and the Land*, 1955
Stamp, L. Dudley and Hoskins, W.G., *The Common Lands of England and Wales*, 1963
Stamp, Sir Dudley, Nature *Conservation in Britain*, 1969
Stratton, J.M., *Agricultural Records*, 1979
Trevelyan, G.M., *English Social History*, 1944
Trevelyan, G.M., *History of England*, 1926
Trow-Smith, Robert, *English Husbandry*, 1961
Wacher, John, *The Towns of Roman Britain*, 1975
Watkins, Alfred, *The Old Straight Track*, 1925
Whitlock, Ralph, *Wiltshire*, 1975
Whitlock, Ralph, *Somerset*, 1976
Whitlock, Ralph, *A Family and a Village*, 1969
Whitlock, Ralph, *Gentle Giants*, 1976
Whitlock, Ralph, *A Short History of British Farming*, 1967
Whitlock, Ralph, *The Warrior Kings of Saxon England*, 1977
Whitlock, Ralph, *A Calendar of Country Customs, 1978*
Wood, Eric S, *Collins' Field Guide to Archaeology*, 1963
Woods, K.S., *Rural Crafts of England*, 1975
Ziegler, Philip, *The Black Death*, 1969

Index